Thomas Jefferson *Redivivus*

THOMAS JEFFERSON REDIVIVUS

Photographs by Joseph C. Farber

Text by Wendell D. Garrett

Barre Publishers

BARRE · MASSACHUSETTS

Frontispiece: *Houdon's marble bust of Jefferson*, 1789. *Museum of Fine Arts, Boston.*

© 1971 by Barre Publishing Co., Inc.

All rights reserved

Library of Congress Catalog Card Number 79–128394

Standard Book Number 8271–7017–3

Designed by Klaus Gemming, New Haven, Connecticut

Printed in the United States of America

TABLE OF CONTENTS

Acknowledgments

THIS BOOK is a collaboration in several ways, not only between the photographer and the author, but also between us and an imaginative publisher, a talented manuscript editor, a creative book designer, and a host of close friends of Mr. Jefferson. Working on it we have been occasionally astonished and continually encouraged in finding that simply the mention of Jefferson's name and an expression of our interest in his republic of ideas have evoked from total strangers instant openhanded aid.

The greatest debt of all we owe to the two foremost Jefferson scholars of our time: Dumas Malone of the University of Virginia and Julian P. Boyd of Princeton University. They are best known through their monumental works, which are still in progress—Malone's multivolume *Jefferson and His Time* and Boyd's meticulously edited *The Papers of Thomas Jefferson*. From these incomparable primary sources all other books on Jefferson, including ours, are derivative and by comparison fragmentary. Intellectually, the author's heaviest debt is to Walter Muir Whitehill of the Boston Athenæum and to L. H. Butterfield of The Adams Papers at the Massachusetts Historical Society, who have long been steadfast friends and wise counselors. In addition it is a pleasure to acknowledge the good wishes of many devoted friends, and the valuable contributions and encouragement of those whose help has ranged from a casual suggestion to tireless footwork at different stages in the book's preparation. It would be incomplete without an expression of appreciation to the following: Mrs. N. Addison Baker of Tuckahoe, James A. Bear Jr. of the Thomas Jefferson Memorial Foundation, Francis L. Berkeley Jr. of the University of Virginia, Mrs. Thomas N. DeLashmutt of Oak Hill, Carl L. Feiss of the National Trust for Historic Preservation, Frederick R. Goff of the Library of Congress, Frederick D. Nichols of the University of Virginia, Joseph F. Johnston of Bremo, and Mrs. James Owen Watts of Poplar Forest. We also wish to express our gratitude to the talented staff members of the curatorial departments of Colonial Williamsburg, the Bibliothèque Municipale, and the Museum of Fine Arts in Boston, who were unfailing in their courtesy and cooperation. The photographer would like to express his appreciation to Edward Steichen for his inspiration and early guidance.

We are deeply appreciative to Gail Stewart for her painstaking editorial scrutiny of the typescript. Her keen eye, quiet voice, sharp pencil, and penetrating suggestions have improved the book's structure and thought at every stage. The typographical art of Klaus Gemming in the book's design has been indispensable and speaks for itself. The manuscript was prepared with skill and cheerful dispatch by Dorothy Ellesin, who offered suggestions of more than routine importance.

We can conclude these acknowledgments only by paying tribute to the devoted collaboration of our wives, Caroline Farber and Jane Garrett, who shared with us the trials of composition and picture editing, and made many helpful suggestions in matters of style and tone.

WENDELL GARRETT
JOSEPH FARBER

Introduction

THERE was prophetic truth in the dying words of John Adams: "Thomas Jefferson still survives." Jefferson is the one American statesman who is timeless: not only is he the central, most familiar figure in American history, but he also is, of all the Founding Fathers, indeed of all the men of the eighteenth century, the most contemporary. It is above all his brilliant formulation and championship of the fundamental doctrines of human freedom and individual liberty that make him as relevant today as he was in the eighteenth century. Freedom, he wrote, "is the most sacred cause that ever man was engaged in." Without the "precious blessing" of liberty, he said, life has no sense and no dignity. Lincoln better than anyone else comprehended the basic ideas of democracy's most outspoken champion when he wrote, "The principles of Jefferson are the definitions and axioms of a free society."

No leader in the period of the American Enlightenment was as articulate, as wise, as conscious of the implications and consequences of a free society as he. To the end of his life his opinions on many subjects varied as his experience ripened—but he never wavered in his faith in government of the people by and for themselves, holding that "the people are the only sure reliance for the preservation of our liberty." He held that all men are created equal, that they possess certain inalienable rights, and that governments derive their just powers from the consent of the governed. That unwavering trust in the dependability, wisdom, and honesty of the common literate individual is his greatest legacy. Woodrow Wilson once said, "The immortality of Thomas Jefferson does not lie in any one of his achievements, but in his attitude toward mankind."

Jefferson was, of course, quite beyond any of his contemporaries—Franklin perhaps excepted—in the breadth of his interests, his studies, and his skills. He stands out as the one clear figure in our early history—a perfect Doric column. He was not merely a statesman of the first order, but a very principal in the domain of original thought and moral force. There had never been, in all probability, a mind like his since the Italian Renaissance. He learned many languages, built one of the great eighteenth-century libraries, and was warmly claimed by the French intellectuals as a fellow *philosophe*. No one has yet exhausted the richness of that mind: philosopher and scientist, inventor and architect, linguist and educator, farmer and horticulturist, man of letters and bibliophile, classicist and lawyer, musician and indefatigable letter-writer, diplomatist and philosophical statesman—he was a true son of the eighteenth century. Even in an age of versatility, his scientific attainments, his wide scholarship and extraordinary learning, his skill in mechanics and architecture, his almost universal curiosity, are a matter of perpetual astonishment. Nor were all these interests—so abundantly revealed in his writings—simply the expression of dilettantism. Whatever he learned, whatever he knew, fitted into and enriched his philosophy. To every field he brought a fresh, inquiring mind; in each he left an imprint which pushed ahead the frontiers of human knowledge.

A curious, inexplicable quality of elusiveness, however, hovers over the reputation of

Jefferson. This is due in part to the subtlety of his mind; but in a far deeper way his life reveals a congeries of bewildering conflicts and contradictions. His contemporaries by their own accounts found him easy to know but impossible to know well. Albert J. Nock has observed, "He was the most approachable and the most impenetrable of men, easy and delightful of acquaintance, impossible of knowledge." Aristocratic by birth and inclination, he became the first great democrat, the people's friend; dedicated to his native land, he was more cosmopolitan than national in thought and feeling, more at home among the classical ruins in Europe than on the impoverished American frontier; scholarly and reclusive by taste and training, he was popular with the masses; acutely sensitive to personal criticism and party strife, he was the chosen instrument of American democracy. "Jefferson," Carl Becker concluded, "was a democrat by intellectual conviction, but by temperament and training a Virginia aristocrat." He embodied the essential ambivalence built into the social and political life of America. He can be properly visualized only in both dimensions of the paradox. In his *History of the United States*,

Henry Adams wrote with perception: "Almost every other American statesman might be described in a parenthesis. A few broad strokes of the brush would paint the portrait of all the early presidents with this exception . . . Jefferson could be painted only touch by touch, with a fine pencil."

For forty years, from 1769 to 1809, Thomas Jefferson was a towering figure in American politics, passing through the offices of Virginia legislator, representative to the Continental Congress, governor of his state, ambassador to France, secretary of state, vice-president, and finally, from 1801 to 1809, president of the United States. For sixteen more years his close associates James Madison and James Monroe occupied the White House. Yet it was not politics, but that moral freedom which had animated democracy from the ancient Greeks to modern representative government in his own day that had always been his cherished ideal. Only in defense of the rights of the individual was he intolerant, and in the battle for them he neither asked nor gave quarter. "I have sworn upon the altar of god," he said, "eternal hostility against every form of tyranny over the mind of man."

Thomas Jefferson *Redivivus*

CHAPTER I

YOUTH
AND EDUCATION
(1743–1767)

THOMAS JEFFERSON *was born a British subject at Shadwell, a modest frame house in Albemarle County, Virginia, on April 13 (April 2, Old Style), 1743. Four miles away was the village of Charlottesville, and a mile and a half distant, across the fields, was the mountain on which he was to build the mansion he would call Monticello. Shadwell, finely situated in a clearing on a slight rise of ground on the north bank of the Rivanna, a little above its junction with the James River, was the most important of several tobacco plantations carved out of the savage wilderness in the foot-hills of the Blue Ridge Mountains by his father.*

Peter Jefferson was a vigorous and intelligent man, a tender and warmhearted man, of modest birth, self-made and self-educated, whose "education had been quite neglected," but, as his son wrote, "being of a strong mind, sound judgment and eager after information, he read much and improved himself insomuch that he was chosen with Joshua Fry, professor of Mathem. in W. & M. college, to continue the boundary line between Virginia and N. Carolina." The Jefferson and Fry "Map of Inhabited Parts of Virginia" was compiled in 1751; by this time Peter Jefferson was the wealthiest and most respected squire of the

county. Having mastered the art of surveying, he became a deputy surveyor of Albemarle County, magistrate, justice of the peace, sheriff, colonel of the militia, and member of the Virginia House of Burgesses.

When Peter Jefferson died on August 17, 1757, he left his fourteen-year-old son not only valuable lands and property but also the cherished memory of a Gibraltar-like parent: a vigorous frontiersman of prodigious physical strength, a hard-working, God-fearing, and affectionate father. He was one of those rugged and hard-muscled men who opened the wilderness to civilization by their strength and courage. Years later, Jefferson recalled that upon his father's death, the "whole care & direction of myself was thrown on myself entirely, without a relation or friend qualified to advise or guide me." As an impressionable boy, Thomas Jefferson inherited from his father the qualities of generosity and kindness, and from him he learned respect for truth and love of knowledge, as well as severe intellectual discipline and physical endurance; the father taught the son to ride, to shoot, to hunt, and to canoe on the Rivanna; he also taught him to read, to write, to keep accounts, and to work systematically. In his Autobiography he related something about his first exposure to

Shadwell, the site of Jefferson's birthplace.

systematic schooling, at the prompting of his father, who, denied a formal education himself, was careful to direct that his son be given the classical training he had missed:

He placed me at the English school at 5. years of age and at the Latin at 9. where I continued until his death. My teacher Mr. Douglas a clergyman from Scotland was but a superficial Latinist, less instructed in Greek, but with the rudiments of these languages he taught me French, and on the death of my father I went to the revd. Mr. Maury a correct classical scholar, with whom I continued two years.

The education of the young Jefferson was such a happy experience that late in life he said, if he were called upon to choose between the large estate left him by his father and the education given him, he would choose the latter without hesitation. When he left the school of the Scotchman, the Reverend William Douglas, he left with memories of "mouldy pies and excellent instruction."

It was during his boyhood that Thomas Jefferson became acquainted personally with Indians, who found a friend in his father and stopped to visit Shadwell for advice and hospitality on their way to Williamsburg. As a county colonel, Peter Jefferson was responsible for the preservation of order on the Indian frontier; he kept the peace by making friends and playing fair with them. Years afterward, Thomas Jefferson, who shared his father's admiration for these Indians, recalled in a letter to John Adams in 1812:

So much in answer to your enquiries concerning Indians, a people with whom, in the very early part of my life, I was very familiar, and acquired impressions of attachment and

commiseration for them which have never been obliterated. Before the revolution they were in the habit of coming often, and in great numbers to the seat of our government, where I was very much with them. I knew much of the great Outassete, the warrior and orator of the Cherokees. He was always the guest of my father, on his journeys to and from Williamsburg. I was in his camp when he made his great farewell oration to his people, the evening before his departure for England. The moon was in full splendor, and to her he seemed to address himself in his prayers for his own safety on the voyage, and that of his people during his absence. His sounding voice, distinct articulation, animated action, and the solemn silence of his people at their several fires, filled me with awe and veneration, altho' I did not understand a word he uttered.

Later, when that chief's people were threatened with extermination, Jefferson, with his memory of that moonlight night perpetually fresh in his memory, exerted a heroic effort to save them.

Jane Randolph, Thomas Jefferson's mother, a refined and accomplished daughter of Isham Randolph, was twenty-three when he was born—her third child in three years, the other two being girls. She eventually gave birth to ten children, some of whom died young; when Peter Jefferson died, the family consisted of Thomas and an infant brother, Randolph, and seven women—the mother and six sisters. Even though his mother survived his father by a good many years, Jefferson maintained what was close to an impenetrable silence about her in his letters: the rare references to his mother which do exist are curiously dry and curt.

The Randolphs were rich and easily ranked among the first families of Virginia. Jefferson

Shadwell on the Rivanna with Monticello in the distance.

was proud of the sturdy yeomanry and stock of his father and boasted of his humble origin, but remarked in his Autobiography, *with a laconic contempt for the lineage of the Randolphs,* "They trace their pedigree far back in England & Scotland, to which let every one ascribe the faith & merit he chooses." *He knew little about his ancestors:* "The tradition of my father's family was that their ancestor came to this country from Wales, and from near the mountain of Snowdon, the highest in Gr. Br."

He had in his veins the blood of the two Virginias—the aristocracy of the Tidewater and the yeomanry of the Piedmont; the sensitive pride and refinement of the Randolphs united with the physical strength and inexhaustible energy of mind and capacity for improving opportunities which accounted for the rise of his father; the reckless prodigality and pretentious living of the rich planters, and the belligerently independent and instinctively democratic traits of the old yeomanry.

Jefferson's contempt for aristocrats and for those who claimed special dispensations persisted as one of his most enduring prejudices. With a touch of irony and a bit of hostility, he wrote Thomas Adams, his London agent, in 1771 and requested him

to search the Herald's office for the arms of my family. I have what I have been told were the family arms, but on what authority I know not. It is possible there may be none. If so I would with your assistance become a purchaser, having Sterne's word for it that a coat of arms may be purchased as cheap as any other coat.

Peter Jefferson—who would have appreciated this independent stance of mind in his son —at around the age of twenty-five had become a close friend of Colonel William Randolph, the wealthy and aristocratic owner of the fine plantation of Tuckahoe on the James River, located a few miles from Richmond. It was William's cousin, Jane, that Peter met and married in October 1739, when he was thirty-one and she was nineteen, after he had cleared a thousand acres and built his house, Shadwell, on the Rivanna. As he could find no site upon his own farm suitable for a residence, he persuaded his intimate friend, Colonel Randolph, who owned 4,300 acres adjoining, to

Tuckahoe, the house of William Randolph.

Entrance to Tuckahoe, Goochland County, near Richmond, Virginia. It was here that Jefferson spent his childhood and received his early education in a nearby schoolhouse.

The Wren Building of the College of William and Mary, Williamsburg, Virginia.
As a youth of seventeen Jefferson came to Williamsburg to study for two years
in the College, after which he read law with George Wythe.

give him a sightly spot on the latter's land; the price of the property was "Henry Weatherbourne's biggest bowl of arrack punch." But Jefferson's early childhood was not to be spent at Shadwell, because the family moved to Tuckahoe in August 1745 after the death of William Randolph. The difference in the style of life and architecture between the rude wilderness frame dwelling, Shadwell, and the more sophisticated plantation house, Tuckahoe, was even greater symbolically than the real distance separating them of fifty mudtracked miles. Jefferson's earliest memories during these formative years of his life were acquired at his adopted home.

Sarah N. Randolph in her Domestic Life of Thomas Jefferson *explained:*

"It was the dying request of Colonel Randolph, that his friend Peter Jefferson should undertake the management of his estates and the guardianship of his young son, Thomas Mann Randolph. Being unable to fulfill this request while living at Shadwell, Colonel Jefferson removed his family to Tuckahoe, and remained there seven years, sacredly guarding, like a Knight of the Round Table, the solemn charge intrusted to him, without any other reward than the satisfaction of fully keeping the promise made to his dying friend. That he refused to receive any other compen-

Secretary's Ford in the Rivanna between Shadwell and Monticello.

Tuckahoe and its schoolhouse, where Jefferson had his first schooling.

sation for his services as guardian is not only proved by the frequent assertion of his son in after years, but by his accounts as executor, which have ever remained unchallenged.

"Thomas Jefferson was not more than two years old when his father moved to Tuckahoe, yet he often declared that his earliest recollection in life was of being, on that occasion, handed up to a servant on horseback, by whom *he was carried on a pillow for a long distance. He also remembered that later, when five years old, he one day became impatient for his school to be out, and, going out, knelt behind the house, and there repeated the Lord's Prayer, hoping thereby to hurry up the desired hour."*

At the age of five Jefferson had been sent to school at Tuckahoe to learn the rudiments of

English; at the age of nine he was placed under the care of the Reverend William Douglas to learn Latin, Greek, French, and mathematics. By the death of his father, Jefferson, at the age of fourteen, was thrown on his own resources and entered a school kept by James Maury, a classical scholar of Huguenot extraction and Whig clergyman with a broad and independent mind, who lived fourteen miles from Shadwell at the foot of Peter's Mountain. He recalled long afterwards this period of his life in a letter to his eldest grandson. Remembering "the various sorts of bad company with which I associated from time to time . . ." he said, "I am astonished that I did not turn off with some of them, and become as worthless to society as they were." For two years he remained under the masterful tutorage of

Maury, working hard at his books and exploring the wild and beautiful frontier, taking abundant exercise, during holidays and vacations. His famous Notes on Virginia, *written in 1781 and 1782 at Monticello, are full of observations on wild animals which must have been assembled from his boyhood recollections and observations in the primeval forest that stretched out from his home. Many of these tastes and interests of boyhood developed later into serious hobbies and scientific pursuits.*

Two years had passed with Maury when Jefferson in January 1760 spent the night at Peter Randolph's, where they discussed his schooling; he was advised to enter college. He wrote a letter to his guardian, John Harvie, and expressed his reasons for wanting to go:

In the first place as long as I stay at the Mountains the Loss of one fourth of my Time is inevitable, by Company's coming here and detaining me from School. And likewise my Absence will in a great Measure put a Stop to so much Company, and by that Means lessen the Expences of the Estate in House-Keeping. And on the other Hand by going to the College I shall get a more universal Acquaintance, which may hereafter be serviceable to me; and I suppose I can pursue my Studies in Greek and Latin as well there as here, and likewise learn something of the Mathematics.

His father had died three years earlier and the son was taking his responsibilities seriously: here were the characteristics of the man of seventy in the boy of seventeen, with his dislike for wasted time, his desire for financial economy by curtailing hospitality, and his wish to enrich his mind. His guardian consented, and in the spring of 1760, having just turned seventeen, he left Shadwell for Wil-

liamsburg to enter the College of William and Mary.

Williamsburg, the capital of the colonial government of Virginia where Jefferson was to study and work for the next fifteen years, is situated on a neck of land between the York and James rivers only a few miles from where the broad Chesapeake Bay joins the Atlantic. Named in honor of William III, the reigning monarch, in 1699, when it was decided to move the seat of government from the old capital at Jamestown, it was hardly more than a village when Jefferson arrived there, with a population of around a thousand whites and blacks—a population that rose and fell according to whether the legislature was in session or in recess.

But small though the little capital may appear to us, it was nevertheless the political, social, and cultural center of the Tidewater; to the tall, gangling, redheaded boy from Shadwell it was something of a metropolis with a giddy social life. Williamsburg was no ordinary village in the mid-eighteenth century; few early American towns offered as much high life and fashion, as much dissipation and round of pleasures, cards and dice, horse racing and cockfighting, balls and plays. Into this dizzy pool of pleasure Jefferson plunged in his late teens, and looking back years later wondered how he survived:

From the circumstances of my position, I was often thrown into the society of horse racers, card players, fox hunters, scientific and professional men, and of dignified men; and many a time have I asked myself, in the enthusiastic moment of the death of a fox, the victory of a favorite horse, the issue of a question eloquently argued at the bar, or in the great council of the nation, well, which of these kinds of reputation should I prefer?

The Palace, the residence for governors in Williamsburg.

That of a horse jockey? a fox hunter? an orator? or the honest advocate of my country's rights? . . .

I had the good fortune to become acquainted very early with some characters of very high standing, and to feel the incessant wish that I could ever become what they were. Under temptations and difficulties, I would ask myself what would Dr. Small, Mr. Wythe, Peyton Randolph do in this situation? I am certain that this mode of deciding on my conduct, tended more to its correctness than any reasoning powers I possessed.

The central axis and favorite promenade of the town was the Duke of Gloucester Street, a hundred feet wide. At head end stood the three or four buildings of the College of William and Mary in brick, designed by Sir Christopher Wren in the style of Chelsea Hospital; the Burgesses met there until the first state house or capitol was completed in 1705 at the foot of the Duke of Gloucester and within view of the college. A "palace" for the royal governor was soon built between the college and the capitol to the side. This tight little triangle— college, capitol, and palace—formed the periphery of Thomas Jefferson's world for the years of his youth.

On this main stem Bruton Parish Church was built (now thought to be the oldest Episcopal church in this country) in order to provide the inhabitants a place of worship in the mode of the established religion. Also along this street were some fine, if not pretentious, houses, that were noted for their taste, hospitality, and profusion of elegant furniture. Taverns, shops, and a courthouse completed the principal buildings. An inn, appropriately called the Raleigh Tavern, was a festive scene, where distinguished lawyers attending court or the legislature drank with abandon and

danced the quadrilles and minuets through the night. The Apollo Room of the Raleigh Tavern, later destined to a conspicuous page in the history of the American Revolution because of its setting for momentous political stratagems of the Virginia Whigs, was the scene of Jefferson's stumbling marriage proposal to Rebecca Burwell, his "Belinda."

Thomas Jefferson entered the College of William and Mary on March 25, 1760. Even though the school was poorly governed and equipped, staffed in large part by mediocre teachers and filled with rowdy, pleasure-bent students—"rife with dissensions and discontent," in the words of one of the college's historians—it proved to be the training ground in this era of some of the most prominent architects of American independence and the American republic. Jefferson was at a susceptible age —a fatherless boy, wealthy, flattered, a bold sportsman, throbbing with the joy of life, and surrounded by gaiety and recklessness—and it appears from his letters that he did have some boyish escapades in his first year. He found he had spent too much on dress and horses, for example, and wrote his guardian in remorse that, since his college bills seemed to be excessive, his whole expenditure for the year in Williamsburg should be charged to his separate share of the property. "No," was the reply, "if you have sowed your wild oats in this way, the estate can well afford to pay the bill."

It is obvious that Jefferson had already matured intellectually more than his peers by this period in his educational career; he was spurred on by a passion for knowledge, combined with an insatiable thirst and taste for letters, arts, and science. And fortunately for him, there was an exceptional teacher at William and Mary who had a profound influence in the molding of Jefferson's mind and character, and, in the end, his career: this man,

William Small, a Scot of great learning who was professor of natural philosophy and mathematics, arrived at the college about the same time that Jefferson came as a student. Long afterward the student in his Autobiography *paid a moving tribute to the Scottish professor:*

I . . . went to Wm. and Mary college, to wit in the spring of 1760, where I continued 2. years. It was my great good fortune, and what probably fixed the destinies of my life, that Dr. Wm. Small of Scotland was then professor of Mathematics, a man profound in most of the useful branches of science, with a happy talent of communication correct and gentlemanly manners, & an enlarged and liberal mind. He, most happily for me, became soon attached to me & made me his daily companion when not engaged in the school; and from his conversation I got my first views of the expansion of science & of the system of things in which we are placed. Fortunately the Philosophical chair became vacant soon after my arrival at college, and he was appointed to fill it per interim: and he was the first who ever gave in that college regular lectures in Ethics, Rhetoric & Belles lettres. He returned to Europe in 1762 [i.e., 1764], having previously filled up the measure of his goodness to me, by procuring for me, from his most intimate friend G. Wythe, a reception as a student of law, under his direction, and introduced me to the acquaintance and familiar table of Governor Fauquier, the ablest man who had ever filled that office. With him, and at his table, Dr. Small & Mr. Wythe, his amici omnium horarum, & myself, formed a partie quarree, & to the habitual conversations on these occasions I owed much instruction.

Perhaps the greatest man among this intimate circle of friends, and perhaps the man who was to have the most lasting influence on Jefferson, was George Wythe, professor of law at the college and the foremost jurist in colonial Virginia. Of him Jefferson said:

The Wythe House in Williamsburg, built about 1750.

No man ever left behind him a character more venerated than George Wythe. His virtue was of the purest tint; his integrity inflexible, and his justice exact; of warm patriotism, and, devoted as he was to liberty, and the natural and equal rights of man, he might truly be called the Cato of his country, without the avarice of the Roman; for a more disinterested person never lived. Temperance and regularity in all his habits, gave him general good health, and his unaffected modesty and suavity of manners endeared him to everyone. He was of easy elocution, his language chaste, method-ical in the arrangement of his matter, learned and logical in the use of it, and of great urbanity in debate; not quick of apprehension, but, with a little time, profound in penetration, and sound in conclusion. In his philosophy he was firm, and neither troubling, nor perhaps trusting, anyone with his religious creed, he left the world to the conclusion, that religion must be good which could produce a life of such exemplary virtue. . . .

Mr. Wythe continued to be my faithful and beloved Mentor in youth, and my most affectionate friend through life.

Chess room in the Wythe House.

The Wythe House study.

If Jefferson found in Small the philosopher and professor and in Wythe the lawyer and lawgiver, he found in Governor Francis Fauquier the elegant and accomplished man of the world: half a century later, the great democrat Jefferson remembered the gentlemanly royalist Governor Fauquier as "the ablest man who had ever filled that office." This coterie of intellectual leaders in Williamsburg proved to be a veritable university to Jefferson: from Small he learned the habit of thinking for himself, from Wythe the meaning of scholarship, and from Fauquier the pleasure of manners. Fauquier was an open-minded and open-hearted eighteenth-century gentleman, interested in new ideas and good talk; Jefferson spent much time in the governor's company and learned many things that were to be avoided and much that was to be imitated.

At these dinners I have heard more good sense, more rational and philosophical conversations, than in all my life besides. They were truly Attic societies. The Governor was musical also, and a good performer, and associated me with two or three other amateurs in his weekly concerts.

Dr. Small quit the college and departed for England in 1764 under disagreeable circumstances involving administration policies, and so after two years this intimate circle of friends was broken. For Jefferson the heart of the college was now gone. Yet, he did not stand aloof from his classmates. He formed many close associations with his classmates, most of whom were the sons of the middle gentry from central and western Virginia. All of his fellow students agreed on Jefferson's remarkable appli-

Musicians' corner of the Apollo Room, Raleigh Tavern, Williamsburg.

cation to his studies; John Page recalled that he himself had never "made any great proficiency in any study, for I was too sociable, and fond of the conversation of my friends, to study as Mr. Jefferson did, who could tear himself away from his dearest friends, to fly to his studies." He studied with intense absorption, sometimes for as long as fifteen hours a day, and robust enough to find his exercise by running a mile out of Williamsburg and back.

But Jefferson was a young Virginia gentleman of spirit, and hard studies and youthful pleasures were mixed in his student years. Society in Williamsburg moved at a fast pace and sometimes he would refer to the gay college town as "Devilsburg." His intense moral sense and distaste for loafing diminished the pleasure that his average fellow students would have found in dissipation. Jefferson participated in these pleasures sparingly. He never used tobacco, never played cards, never fought, and rarely drank, but he did enjoy the innocent gaiety of riding, fiddling, singing, dancing, flirting with the girls, and playing "at ye billiard tables." Once after a binge with some fellow students, he wrote "the morning after" on October 7, 1763, from the depths of despair to his intimate friend John Page:

In the most melancholy fit that ever any poor soul was, I sit down to write to you. Last night, as merry as agreeable company and dancing with Belinda in the Apollo could make me, I never could have thought the succeeding sun would have seen me so wretched as I now am! I was prepared to say a great deal: I had dressed up in my own mind, such thoughts as occurred to me, in as moving a language as I knew how, and expected to have performed in a tolerably creditable manner. But, good God! When I had an opportunity of venting them, a few broken sentences, uttered in great disorder, and interrupted with pauses of uncommon length, were the too visible marks of my strange confusion! The whole confab I will tell you, word for word, if I can, when I see you, which God send may be soon.

Two years of intense application to his studies exhausted any future potentialities of the College of William and Mary for Jefferson, particularly after Dr. Small's departure. He was nineteen and on Small's advice he settled down to his study of the law in the chambers of George Wythe. Wythe, then thirty-five years of age, was unquestionably the most learned and scholarly lawyer in all Virginia; it was said of him that "in the solid learning of the law he stood, with the exception of Thomson Mason, almost alone." An impressive and convincing speaker, his thoughts and arguments were prepared with the greatest care; Jefferson once said of him, that "in pleading he never indulged himself with a useless or a declamatory word." Master and student had numerous mental qualities in common. That Wythe was a great influence on Jefferson's early career there can be little doubt. He was "my second father," Jefferson declared, "my antient master, my earliest & best friend; and to him I am indebted for first impressions

which have had the most salutary influence on the course of my life."

With characteristic pertinacity and thoroughness of purpose, Jefferson applied himself to an incredible regimen of studies. Not long after he began the practice of law, he drew up an outline or timetable of study for students of the law which was undoubtedly based on the method he himself had followed. The ideal routine begins at dawn and ends at bedtime, without time for either meals or recreation. From eight to twelve he suggested solid reading of the law and proposed a method for assimilation:

In reading the reporters, enter in a commonplace book every case of value, condensed into the narrowest possible compass which will admit of presenting distinctly the principle of the case. This operation is doubly useful, insomuch as it obliges the student to seek out the pith of the case, and habituates him to a condensation of thought and to an acquisition of the most valuable of all the talents, that of never using two words when one will do.

He exhorted young neophytes not merely to the study of law, but to an astonishing range of reading in Latin, French, mathematics, natural philosophy, ethics, natural religion, politics, history, belles-lettres, rhetoric, and oratory. He clearly believed of the lawyer, what Cicero believed of the orator, that he should know something of all knowledge.

It was during his days under the watchful eye of Wythe that Jefferson set a high standard for himself and began keeping his own commonplace book in which he followed his own suggestions. Five years after he had retired from the presidency he wrote his friend Thomas Cooper how he kept his notes and recorded observations during his years as a law student in pre-Revolutionary Williamsburg:

When I was a student of the law . . . after getting through Coke-Littleton, whose matters cannot be abridged, I was in the habit of abridging and commonplacing what I read, meriting it, and of sometimes mixing my own reflections on the subject. . . . They were written at a time of life when I was bold in the pursuit of knowledge, never fearing to follow truth and reason to whatever results they led, and bearding every authority which stood in their way.

In 1767, after he had had five years of apprenticeship study of the law, his teacher and mentor, George Wythe, led him before the General Court of Virginia, where, after examination into his qualifications, he was admitted to the bar. Considering the years of intensive research and grueling labor he devoted to his preparation, few American lawyers could have entered the practice so thoroughly and soundly equipped. Indeed, the surprising thing about his legal preparation was that it took so long; five years of study was practically unheard of for young men at the law in the eighteenth century—two years was considered more than ample, and in many cases a year or less was deemed sufficient.

The newly fledged lawyer was now twenty-four and one of the richest young men in Virginia; he settled down to the practice of his profession, maintaining an office in Williamsburg though spending much time at Shadwell personally superintending his own lands and crops as well as those of his mother. He was gaining the reputation of being the most learned and the most inquisitive young man in the colony. A woman writing from Williamsburg about this time related that she "never knew any one to ask so many questions as Thomas Jefferson."

CHAPTER II

THE BUSINESS OF LIFE
(1767-1774)

WHEN *Thomas Jefferson began to practice law at the age of twenty-four, he was brilliantly prepared for his profession. He obtained business in reasonable volume, handling routine cases for a country lawyer—land contracts, slanders, the trespassing of stock, the defense or challenging of wills, the administration of estates, suits on securities, and occasional cases of assault and battery. He rode the circuit to various county seats and handled matters that brought him in contact with illuminating aspects of Virginia life and manners. He was a hard-working young lawyer and his practice grew rapidly. At the time Jefferson disposed of his law practice before the outbreak of the American Revolution and entered the field of practical politics, his annual income from the law alone mounted to the equivalent of about $3,000 a year. Nothing Jefferson undertook could be mediocre, and it is not surprising that he became a successful lawyer. Famous clients, such as Burwells, Byrds, Lord Fairfax, Harrisons, Lees, Nelsons, Pages, and Randolphs, sought his services, and distinguished lawyers consulted him.*

The legal profession did not occupy Jefferson's attention exclusively, however; between law cases and overseeing the plantation at Shadwell, he read voluminously and led an active social life, especially when he was in Williamsburg. Items in his account books for these years indicate that he found time to play his violin, and to attend shooting matches, concerts, puppet shows, and the theater at Williamsburg. But his chief passion was architecture. The young man of twenty-five dreamed of a country house of classical architectural distinction to outshine anything in the Georgian colonies. Toward the end of 1767 he actually began work on his villa. Lumber was sawed into planks, glass was ordered for windows, and contracts made to level the top of the highest summit on his estate, just across the Rivanna River from his birthplace, and in March 1769 to plant a variety of fruit trees on the slope.

He was still living at Shadwell when he began to carry into effect the dream of his youth: to build a house for himself on the crest of the hill, which he was to call Monticello after the Italian for "the little mountain," adapting elements from the architectural treatises of Andrea Palladio, the renowned Italian architect of the sixteenth century who based his designs on the ancient Roman villas and country houses. By 1768 he had acquired the notable volume of Palladio entitled Four Books of Architecture. *In his artistic and literary tastes,*

THE
ARCHITECTURE
OF
A. PALLADIO;
IN FOUR BOOKS.

CONTAINING

A short TREATISE of the FIVE ORDERS, and
the most necessary Observations concerning
all sorts of BUILDING:

AS ALSO

The different Construction of PRIVATE and PUBLICK HOUSES,
HIGH-WAYS, BRIDGES, MARKET-PLACES, XYSTES, and
TEMPLES, with their Plans, Sections, and Uprights.

Revis'd, Design'd, and Publish'd

By *GIACOMO LEONI*, a *Venetian*,
Architect to His Most SERENE HIGHNESS, the Late
ELECTOR PALATINE.

Translated from the ITALIAN *Original.*

THE THIRD EDITION, CORRECTED.

With NOTES and REMARKS of
INIGO JONES:

Now first taken from his Original Manuscript in *Worcester* College Library, *Oxford.*

AND ALSO,

An APPENDIX, containing the ANTIQUITIES of *ROME.*
Written by *A. PALLADIO.*

And a DISCOURSE of the FIRES of the Ancients.
Never before Translated.

IN TWO VOLUMES.

LONDON:

Printed for A. WARD, in *Little-Britain*; S. BIRT, in *Ave-Mary-Lane*; D. BROWNE,
without *Temple-Bar*; C. DAVIS, in *Pater-noster-Row*; T. OSBORNE, in
Gray's-Inn; and A. MILLAR, against St. *Clement's* Church in the *Strand.*

M. DCC. XLII.

Leoni's edition of Andrea Palladio's Four Books of Architecture:
*"there never was a Palladio here even in private hands until I
bought one."*

*Jefferson was essentially a classicist; yet, at the
same time, he was not a slavish imitator of
Palladio. Even as Palladio had modified ancient Roman models to conform to sixteenth-
century Italian conditions, so his young disciple altered and added to his designs to meet
the needs of eighteenth-century Virginia. He
prepared the plans for the mansion in detail;
it would be a quarter century before his "poem
in brick and mortar"—as Claude G. Bowers
was to call it—was finished, but by the fall of*

1769 *a one-room small brick building on the
south end of the terrace was ready for occu-
pancy. As it turned out, he had begun his
building none too soon.*

*On February 1, 1770, disaster struck: Shad-
well, his birthplace, and the home of his mother, sisters, and younger brother, was burned
to the ground. He was a few miles away on
business in Charlottesville, the county seat.
His law books, his records and memoranda of
law cases, his family records and papers, his
letters, notes, and his solid beginnings of a
library were all reduced to ashes. This was an
irretrievable loss. Only his violin and his small
pocket account books seem to have escaped the
flames. His concern was for his books and papers; he lamented his fate in a letter of February 21 to John Page.*

My late loss may perhaps have reac[hed
y]ou by this time, I mean the loss of my mother's house by fire, and in it, of every pa[per I]
had in the world, and almost every book. On a
reasonable estimate I calculate th[e cost o]f
t[he b]ooks burned to have been £200. ster-
ling. Would to god it had been the money
[;then] had it never cost me a sigh! To make
the loss more sensible it fell principally on m[y
books] of common law, of which I have but
one left, at that time lent out. Of papers too of
every kind I am utterly destitute. All of these,
whether public or private, of business or of
amusement have perished in the flames. I had
made some progress in preparing for the succeeding general court, and having, as was my
custom, thrown my thoughts into the form of
notes, I troubled my head no more with them.
These are gone, and 'like the baseless fabric of
a vision, Leave not a trace behind.'

*He could not live or work without books; he
began collecting again at a furious pace and*

The fields below Monticello.

by August 1773, according to his diary, he possessed a new library of 1,254 volumes.

The fire at Shadwell hastened work on his new home on the mountaintop. Into the single room at Monticello, "which, like the cobler's, serves me for parlour for kitchen and hall. I may add, for bed chamber and study too," he moved on November 26, 1770. In a letter of February 20, 1771, he observed, "My friends sometimes take a temperate dinner with me and then retire to look for beds elsewhere. I have hopes however of getting more elbow room this summer." By the time he moved to Monticello he was becoming one of the leading figures of his native Albemarle County: an established lawyer, the owner of considerable landed property, honored by the Royal Government with a commission as "Chief Commander of His Majesty's Horse and Foot" in Albemarle County, appointed by his college surveyor of his county, and chosen by his people as their spokesman in the House of Burgesses. He seemed to his friends to be a perennial bachelor. But not for long.

Sometime in 1770, when he was twenty-seven, he met and quietly fell in love with a beautiful, much-courted widow of twenty-one. She was Martha Wayles Skelton, who lived with her father on his fine estate, The Forest, on the banks of the James River in Charles City County, not far from Williamsburg. Her husband, Bathurst Skelton, had died in September 1768, about two years after their marriage, leaving her with an infant son. No portrait of her has survived; according to memories of her family she was a little above medium height, slight in frame, with a brilliant complexion, hazel eyes, auburn-tinged hair, and "with a lithe and exquisitely formed figure, with a graceful and queenlike carriage." Besides beauty she had other merits. She was better educated than the average young lady in co-

lonial Virginia, she read more widely than her contemporaries, and from her father she inherited a capacity for business: he entrusted her with the keeping of the plantation accounts. But nothing appealed more to Jefferson than her love of music and her accomplishments as a musician. In June 1771 he wrote Thomas Adams, his business agent in London:

I must alter one article in the invoice. I wrote therein for a Clavichord. I have since seen a Forte-piano and am charmed with it. Send me this instrument then instead of the Clavichord. Let the case be of fine mahogany, solid, not vineered. The compass from Double G. to F. in alt. a plenty of spare strings; and the workmanship of the whole very handsome, and worthy the acceptance of a lady for whom I intend it.

Martha did not discourage Jefferson's shy wooing during the spring and winter of 1771, as he became a regular visitor at The Forest. In August 1771, more than a year after he met Martha, he confessed to a friend:

Offer prayers for me too at that shrine to which, tho' absent, I pay continual devotion. In every scheme of happiness she is placed in the fore-ground of the picture, as the principal figure. Take that away, and it is no picture for me.

Toward the end of 1771 Martha Skelton agreed to marry Jefferson and on New Year's Day 1772 the wedding was solemnized at The Forest. For the next decade, until Jefferson suffered the crushing blow of the untimely death of his wife in September 1782, he was the master of his destiny: the proprietor of broad acres, related to the best families of Virginia, and admired and appreciated as a bril-

The Apollo Room of the Raleigh Tavern on the Duke of Gloucester Street, Williamsburg.
In 1773, five patriots, including Jefferson, secretly gathered here to consider closer
cooperation among the colonies.

Independence Hall, Philadelphia.

liant and sound advisor on public affairs. Lord North's seemingly more tolerant policy toward the colonies during the political lull of the early 1770's resulted in an era of good feelings that required little activity in the Virginia House of Burgesses. This long interlude gave Jefferson a chance to devote his time and attention to his marriage, the building of Monticello, and his law practice. He found time to extend his reading and research in widely scattered fields, and his fame as a book collector was beginning to spread.

On his mountaintop Jefferson was passionately devoted to agriculture; he jotted down with unflagging zest precise and minute records of all the incidents of vegetable life in his garden and on his farm from the first leaf in the spring to the day in the fall when his wheat was ready for the sickle. He usually read and wrote in the morning, and spent the early hours of the afternoon on horseback directing his field servants and conferring with his overseers about his tobacco crops. He was a bold and graceful horseman and kept horses of the best blood of the Old Virginia stock, for riding was his favorite exercise. His farm was a large complex of scattered fields and pastures, orchards and gardens, mills and workshops, which demanded his close attention. Jefferson always gave his occupation as that of a farmer, in spite of his versatility and accomplishments as a statesman, lawyer, diplomatist, architect, and philosopher.

These were the bright days of his young manhood when everything seemed to promise happiness and prosperity: married to a lovely wife, building the house of his dreams, collecting afresh his library, and receiving an ample income from his law practice and expanding acres. Regularly and almost routinely he was reelected during the political lull of 1771 to 1773 to the House of Burgesses for each suc-

ceeding session. On the death of his father-in-law, John Wayles, in May 1773, Jefferson's own land holdings were increased twofold.

For a variety of reasons—among them the expanding responsibilities of managing his farms (scattered over three counties), building his house, and participating in the growing political ferment of 1773 and 1774—Jefferson decided to give up the practice of law and turn over his clients to Edmund Randolph in August 1774. The pot of imperial relations between the mother country and the colonies was beginning to boil up in the spring of 1773. Following the inept handling of the Gaspee affair in Rhode Island by British officials, Jefferson and other young members of the Virginia Assembly, particularly those from the "back" districts, gathered one evening in a determined

The South Pavilion, the earliest building at Monticello, completed in 1771.

little caucus at the Raleigh Tavern to plot their strategy: it was the first extra-legal representative body to meet in Virginia. The older members from the Tidewater regions were responding to the crisis in too reluctant and cautious a manner to suit these young hotheads. Jefferson not only felt that the colony was confronted with an inexplicable lack of bold leaders in the Assembly, but also found that "our countrymen seemed to fall into a state of insensibility to our situation."

Not thinking our old & leading members up to the point of forwardness & zeal which the times required, Mr. Henry, R. H. Lee, Francis L. Lee, Mr. Carr & myself agreed to meet in the evening in a private room of the Raleigh to consult on the state of things. There may have been a member or two more whom I do not recollect. We were all sensible that the most urgent of all measures was that of coming to an understanding with all the other colonies to consider the British claims as a common cause to all, & to produce an unity of action: and for this purpose that a commee of correspondce in each colony would be the best instrument for intercommunication: and that their first measure would probably be to propose a meeting of deputies from every colony at some central place, who should be charged with the direction of the measures which should be taken by all. We therefore drew up the resolutions which may be seen in Wirt pa 87. . . .

The next event which excited our sympathies for Massachusets was the Boston port bill, by which that port was to be shut up on the 1st of June, 1774. This arrived while we were in session in the spring of that year. The lead in the house on these subjects being no longer left to the older members, Mr. Henry, R. H. Lee, Fr. L. Lee, 3. or 4. other members, whom I do not recollect, and myself, agreeing

that we must boldly take an unequivocal stand in the line with Massachusetts, determined to meet and consult on the proper measures in the council chamber, for the benefit of the library in that room. We were under conviction of the necessity of arousing our people from the lethargy into which they had fallen as to passing events; and thought that the appointment of a day of general fasting & prayer would be most likely to call up & alarm their attention. No example of such a solemnity had existed since the days of our distresses in the war of 55. since which a new generation had grown up. With the help therefore of Rushworth, whom we rummaged over for the revolutionary precedents & forms of the Puritans of that day, preserved by him, we cooked up a resolution, somewhat modernizing their phrases, for appointing the 1st day of June, on which the Port bill was to commence, for a day of fasting, humiliation & prayer, to implore heaven to avert from us the evils of civil war, to inspire us with firmness in support of our rights, and to turn the hearts of the King & parliament to moderation & justice. To give greater emphasis to our proposition, we agreed to wait the next morning on Mr. Nicholas, whose grave & religious character was more in unison with the tone of our resolution and to solicit him to move it. We accordingly went to him in the morning. He moved it the same day; the 1st of June was proposed and it passed without opposition. The Governor dissolved us as usual. We retired to the Apollo as before, agreed to an association, and instructed the commee of correspdce to propose to the corresponding commees of the other colonies to appoint deputies to meet in Congress at such place, *annually*, as should be convenient to direct, from time to time, the measures required by the general interest: and we declared that an attack on any one colony should be considered as an

Dogwood in blossom, Blue Ridge Mountains.

attack on the whole. This was in May. We further recommended to the several counties to elect deputies to meet at Wmsbg the 1st of Aug ensuing, to consider the state of the colony, & particularly to appoint delegates to a general Congress, should that measure be acceded to by the commees of correspdce generally. It was acceded to, Philadelphia was appointed for the place, and the 5th of Sep. for the time of meeting. We returned home, and in our several counties invited the clergy to meet assemblies of the people on the 1st of June, to perform the ceremonies of the day, & to address to them discourses suited to the occasion. The people met generally, with anxiety & alarm in their countenances, and the effect of the day thro' the whole colony was like a shock of electricity, arousing every man & placing him erect & solidly on his centre. They chose universally delegates for the convention. Being elected one for my own county I prepared a draught of instructions to be given to the delegates whom we should send to the Congress, and which I meant to propose at our meeting. In this I took the ground which, from the beginning I had thought the only one orthodox or tenable, which was that the relation between Gr. Br. and these colonies was exactly the same as that of England & Scotland after the accession of James & until the Union, and the same as her present relations with Hanover, having the same Executive chief but no other necessary political connection; and that our emigration from England to this country gave her no more rights over us, than the emigrations of the Danes and Saxons gave to the present authorities of the mother country over England. In this doctrine however I had never been able to get any one to agree with me but Mr. Wythe. . . . I set out for Wmsbg some days before that appointed for our meeting, but was taken ill of a dysentery on the road, & unable to proceed. I sent on therefore to Wmsbg two copies of my draught, the one under cover to Peyton Randolph, who I knew would be in the chair of the convention, the other to Patrick Henry. Whether Mr. Henry disapproved the ground taken, or was too lazy to read it (for he was the laziest man in reading I ever knew) I never learned: but he communicated it to nobody. Peyton Randolph informed the convention he had received such a paper from a member prevented by sickness from offering it in his place, and he laid it on the table for perusal. It was read generally by the members, approved by many, but thought too bold for the present state of things; but they printed it in pamphlet form under the title of *A Summary view of the rights of British America.*

The Summary View *was intended by Jefferson to form the basis of instructions to the delegates from Virginia to the First Continental Congress. Without his knowledge it was printed anonymously and immediately met with widespread diffusion and eager interest among readers. In retrospect, however, it has proven to be much more than that. This celebrated pamphlet, blistering and revolutionary in content, robust and sweeping in style, was a closely reasoned historical and philosophical indictment of both king and Parliament. It was Jefferson's aim, he said, to "set a pace that would bring the front and rear ranks of [his] fellow countrymen together," but his pace was a rapid one: every paragraph of these instructions breathes of independence. This was a unique document—in some respects as important as the Declaration of Independence—that moved Jefferson in one swift step to the forefront of the great pamphleteers of the Revolution. He was discreet in tone, yet the implication of revolution was unmistakable in his conclusion.*

That these are our grievances which we have thus laid before his majesty with that freedom of language and sentiment which becomes a free people, claiming their rights as derived from the laws of nature, and not as the gift of their chief magistrate. Let those flatter, who fear: it is not an American art. To give praise where it is not due, might be well from the venal, but would ill beseem those who are asserting the rights of human nature. They know, and will therefore say, that kings are the servants, not the proprietors of the people. Open your breast Sire, to liberal and expanded thought. Let not the name of George the third be a blot in the page of history. You are surrounded by British counsellors, but remember that they are parties. You have no ministers for American affairs, because you have none taken from among us, nor amenable to the laws on which they are to give you advice. It behoves you therefore to think and to act for yourself and your people. The great principles of right and wrong are legible to every reader: to pursue them requires not the aid of many counsellors. The whole art of government consists in the art of being honest. Only aim to do your duty, and mankind will give you credit where you fail. . . . The god who gave us life, gave us liberty at the same time: the hand of force may destroy, but cannot disjoin them. This, Sire, is our last, our determined resolution: and that you will be pleased to interpose with that efficacy which your earnest endeavors may insure to procure redress of these our great grievances, to quiet the minds of your subjects in British America against any apprehensions of future incroachment, to establish fraternal love and harmony thro' the whole empire, and that that may continue to the latest ages of time, is the fervent prayer of all British America.

The Summary View *was an extraordinary document; it was a bold look forward to idea and fact of separation, of violent revolution, of self-determination, of national destiny. And in it Jefferson demonstrated the "peculiar felicity of expression," as John Adams called it, which would soon earn him the title "the penman of the Revolution."*

Jefferson's own copy of his A Summary View of the Rights of British America.

CHAPTER III

DRAFTSMAN
OF THE DECLARATION
OF INDEPENDENCE
(1774–1767)

Congress *assembled at Philadelphia on September 4, 1774, under the presidency of Peyton Randolph of Virginia, and adjourned in October with a recommendation to the colonies "to discountenance every species of extravagance and dissipation." The storm which had been gathering so fast in 1774 finally broke upon the land in 1775. When the counties organized committees of safety, Jefferson was elected in January 1775 at the head of the list of appointees in Albemarle County. He was one of his county's two representatives to the second convention of Virginia which met at Richmond on March 20, 1775.*

When the convention assembled it was clear that opinion was divided between conservatives who wanted to avoid a rupture with England at any cost and radical patriots who thought that military preparations should be undertaken at once. When the conservatives, mostly elderly men of substance, persuaded the convention to open their declaration with the expression of loyalty "that it is the most ardent wish of this colony (and they are persuaded of the whole continent of North America) to see a speedy return to those halcyon days when we lived a free and happy people," Patrick Henry *sprang to his feet and delivered the fierce and famous outburst which thrilled his audience, including Jefferson, and resounded like a shrill trumpet blast over the continent of America.*

"We must fight" was the burden of his argument in support of a resolution to arm the militia, and then came his final peroration: "Our brethren are already in the field. Why stand we here idle? Is life so dear, or peace so sweet, as to be purchased at the price of chains and slavery? Forbid it, Almighty God! I know not what course others may take; but as for me give me liberty or give me death!" Edmund Randolph, who was also present, recorded that Jefferson "argued closely, profoundly and warmly on the same side" with Henry.

When Lord North's "Conciliatory Proposition" was received in Virginia, Lord Dunmore, who remained in the Governor's Palace in Williamsburg though impotent to arrest the drift of the colony toward the brink of war, convened the House of Burgesses in early July to consider it. As Peyton Randolph, one of the Virginia delegates to Congress, was speaker

Independence Hall, Philadelphia.

Meetinghouse in Newcastle, Delaware, where Jefferson is said to have visited on his way from Virginia to Philadelphia.

cordingly attended, and the tenor of these propositions being generally known, as having been addressed to all the governors, he was anxious that the answer of our assembly, likely to be the first, should harmonize with what he knew to be the sentiments and wishes of the body he had recently left. He feared that Mr. Nicholas, whose mind was not yet up to the mark of the times, would undertake the answer, & therefore pressed me to prepare an answer. I did so, and with his aid carried it through the house with long and doubtful scruples from Mr. Nicholas and James Mercer, and a dash of cold water on it here & there, enfeebling it somewhat, but finally with unanimity or a vote approaching it. This being passed, I repaired immediately to Philadelphia, and conveyed to Congress the first notice they had of it. It was entirely approved there. I took my seat with them on the 21st of June.

As young as he was, Jefferson stepped out onto the national stage of politics with confidence and determination; he was a talented and versatile man of the world. When he entered Congress, James Parton later observed, he could "calculate an eclipse, survey an estate, tie an artery, plan an edifice, try a cause, break a horse, dance a minuet, and play a violin." The fame of this unassuming and straightforward young Virginian had preceded him to Congress. Years later in 1822 John Adams still remembered the first impression the Virginian had made upon him: "Mr. Jefferson came into Congress in June 1775, and brought with him a reputation for literature, science and a happy talent of composition. Writings of his were handed about, remarkable for the peculiar felicity of expression.... Though a silent member in Congress, he was so prompt, frank, explicit and decisive upon committees and in conversation—not even Samuel Adams was

and his presence would be required at Williamsburg, the Richmond Convention recalled him and appointed Jefferson to succeed him on the Virginia delegation. On June 11th Jefferson left Williamsburg to join his fellow delegates at Philadelphia, where the Second Continental Congress was in session. He was now thirty-two years of age; only two members of Congress—John Jay and Edward Rutledge—were younger.

Ld. North's conciliatory propositions, as they were called, had been received by the Governor and furnished the subject for which this assembly was convened. Mr. Randolph ac-

more so—that he soon seized upon my heart."

His pen was soon requisitioned when he was placed on the committee to draw up a "Declaration of the Causes of Taking Up Arms." Congress felt obliged to give to the world the reasons behind the rebellious scenes between New England farmers and British troops at Lexington and Bunker Hill. The rhetoric of Jefferson's draft was too strong and radical for the conservative delegates, so, out of deference to the authority and prestige of John Dickinson of Pennsylvania, who was also on the committee, he gave way and withdrew it. Dickinson then drafted a statement more acceptable to the party of reconciliation, which was adopted and published, even though the last four paragraphs of this final statement were substantially copied from Jefferson.

Our cause is just. Our union is perfect. Our internal Resources are great, and, if necessary, foreign Assistance is undoubtedly attainable. We gratefully acknowledge, as signal Instances of the Divine Favour towards us, that his Providence would not permit us to be called into this severe Controversy, until we were grown up to our present strength, had been previously exercised in warlike Operation, and possessed of the means of defending ourselves. With hearts fortified with these animating Reflections, we most solemnly, before God and the World, declare, that, exerting the utmost Energy of those Powers, which our beneficent Creator hath graciously bestowed upon us, the Arms we have been compelled by our Enemies to assume, we will, in defiance of every Hazard, with unabating Firmness and Perseverence, employ for the preservation of our Liberties; being with one Mind resolved to die Freemen rather than to live Slaves.

Lest this Declaration should disquiet the Minds of our Friends and Fellow-Subjects in any part of the Empire, we assure them that we mean not to dissolve that Union which has so long and happily subsisted between us, and which we sincerely wish to see restored. Necessity has not yet driven us into that desperate Measure, or induced us to excite any other Nation to War against them. We have not raised Armies with ambitious Designs of separating from Great-Britain, and establishing Independent States. We fight not for Glory or for Conquest. We exhibit to Mankind the remarkable Spectacle of a People attacked by unprovoked Enemies, without any imputation or even suspicion of Offence. They boast of their Privileges and Civilization, and yet proffer no milder Conditions than Servitude or Death.

Carpenters' Hall, Philadelphia: the delegates to the First Continental Congress met here.

In our own native Land, in defence of the Freedom that is our Birthright, and which we ever enjoyed till the late Violation of it—for the protection of our Property, acquired solely by the honest Industry of our fore-fathers and ourselves, against Violence actually offered, we have taken up Arms. We shall lay them down when Hostilities shall cease on the part of the Aggressors, and all danger of their being renewed shall be removed, and not before.

With an humble Confidence in the Mercies of the supreme and impartial Judge and Ruler of the Universe, we most devoutly implore his Divine Goodness to protect us happily through this great Conflict, to dispose our Adversaries to reconciliation on reasonable Terms, and thereby to relieve the Empire from the Calamities of civil War.

It has been said that this document was one of the most popular ever adopted by Congress. "It was," according to Jefferson biographer Francis W. Hirst, "read to the troops by their officers, to the populace amid thundering huzzas in every market place, and to religious bodies amid fervent prayers from nearly every pulpit in the Colonies." With an extraordinary sense of fitness in his choice of words, he formulated here the doctrine of Americanism. Jefferson, with matchless skill, had drawn for the nation and the people an ideal picture, portraying them as they yearned to be looked upon by posterity.

In early August Congress adjourned and Jefferson returned to Monticello for a brief visit. Chosen again as a delegate to Congress, he was delayed in his departure by the sad illness and death of a second child, Jane, in early September. He arrived at Philadelphia late in September and resumed his seat, twenty days after the opening of the session, to find the ideological stance of most of the delegates

shifting more nearly to his position. The king had spurned the second petition of Congress, had not even deigned to listen to it, and was overtly making active military preparations for the coercion of the colonists. Philadelphia was bristling like an armed camp with drilling militia companies. News came from the North that Boston was evacuated and Ticonderoga captured and from the South that Norfolk was burned by the British.

Jefferson left Philadelphia abruptly in late December for Monticello, probably because of news of the deteriorating health of his mother; she died on March 31, 1776. He noted her passing with Spartan brevity in his account book: "My mother died about 8. oclock this morning. In the 57th. year of her age." Some of his alarm was also due to the distressing reports of the ravaging of British forces in Virginia; he had written his brother-in-law, Francis Eppes, a frantic letter in November:

I have never received the scrip of a pen from any mortal in Virginia since I left it, nor been able by any enquiries I could make to hear of my family. I had hoped when Mrs. Byrd came I should have heard something of them, but she could tell me nothing about them. The suspense under which I am is too terrible to be endured. If any thing has happened, for god's sake let me know it.

Jefferson remained at home four months before returning to Philadelphia on May 14, 1776. Events were beginning to move at a furious pace and he energetically entered into the work of Congress. Five days after his return news came that the Virginia Convention had passed a resolution instructing its delegates in Congress to support a motion declaring the "United Colonies free and independent States, absolved from all allegiance or depen-

dence upon the Crown or Parliament of Great Britain." John Adams exclaimed: "Every Post and every Day rolls in upon us Independence like a Torrent." Jefferson's boyhood friend, John Page, wrote a letter from Williamsburg in April that arrived in Philadelphia about this time; in the letter he vehemently urged Jefferson: "For God's sake declare the Colonies independent at once, and save us from ruin."

Congress was marking time until Virginia determined on its course; in the meantime it accelerated the train of events by approving on May 15th the resolution which John Adams and Henry Lee had introduced five days earlier, advising the colonies to adopt "such government as shall in the opinion of the representatives of the people, best conduce to the happiness and safety of their constituents in particular and America in general." By the time the text of this resolution reached Virginia, however, that pivotal colony had already acted. Jefferson vividly recounted the exciting sequence of events in his Autobiography:

On the 15th of May, 1776, the convention of Virginia instructed their delegates in Congress to propose to that body to declare the colonies independent of G. Britain, and appointed a commee to prepare a declaration of rights and plan of government.

In Congress, Friday June 7. 1776. The delegates from Virginia moved in obedience to instructions from their constituents that the Congress should declare that these United colonies are & of right ought to be free & independent states, that they are absolved from all allegiance to the British crown, and that all political connection between them & the state of Great Britain is & ought to be, totally dissolved; that measures should be immediately

taken for procuring the assistance of foreign powers, and a Confederation be formed to bind the colonies more closely together.

The house being obliged to attend at that time to some other business, the proposition was referred to the next day, when the members were ordered to attend punctually at ten o'clock.

Saturday June 8. They proceeded to take it into consideration and referred it to a committee of the whole, into which they immediately resolved themselves, and passed that day & Monday the 10th in debating on the subject.

It was argued by Wilson, Robert R. Livingston, E. Rutledge, Dickinson and others.

That tho' they were friends to the measures themselves, and saw the impossibility that we should ever again be united with Gr. Britain, yet they were against adopting them at this time:

That the conduct we had formerly observed was wise & proper now, of deferring to take any capital step till the voice of the people drove us into it:

That they were our power, & without them our declarations could not be carried into effect;

That the people of the middle colonies (Maryland, Delaware, Pennsylva, the Jerseys & N. York) were not yet ripe for bidding adieu to British connection, but that they were fast ripening & in a short time would join in the general voice of America. . . .

That it would not be long before we should receive certain information of the disposition of the French court, from the agent whom we had sent to Paris for that purpose:

That if this disposition should be favorable, by waiting the event of the present campaign, which we all hoped would be successful, we should have reason to expect an alliance on better terms:

That this would in fact work no delay of any effectual aid from such ally, as, from the advance of the season & distance of our situation, it was impossible we could receive any assistance during this campaign:

That it was prudent to fix among ourselves the terms on which we should form alliance, before we declared we would form one at all events:

And that if these were agreed on, & our Declaration of Independence ready by the time our Ambassador should be prepared to sail, it would be as well as to go into that Declaration at this day.

On the other side it was urged by J. Adams, Lee, Wythe, and others

That no gentleman had argued against the policy or the right of separation from Britain, nor had supposed it possible we should ever renew our connection; that they had only opposed its being now declared:

That the question was not whether, by a declaration of independance, we should make ourselves what we are not; but whether we should declare a fact which already exists:

That as to the people or parliament of England, we had alwais been independent of them, their restraints on our trade deriving efficacy from our acquiescence only, & not from any rights they possessed of imposing them, & that so far our connection had been federal only & was now dissolved by the commencement of hostilities:

That as to the King, we had been bound to him by allegiance, but that this bond was now dissolved by his assent to the late act of parliament, by which he declares us out of his protection, and by his levying war on us, a fact which had long ago proved us out of his protection; it being a certain position in law that allegiance & protection are reciprocal, the one ceasing when the other is withdrawn. . . .

And that the only misfortune is that we did not enter into alliance with France six months sooner, as besides opening their ports for the vent of our last year's produce, they might have marched an army into Germany and prevented the petty princes there from selling their unhappy subjects to subdue us.

It appearing in the course of these debates that the colonies of N. York, New Jersey, Pennsylvania, Delaware, Maryland, and South Carolina were not yet matured for falling from the parent stem, but that they were fast advancing to that state, it was thought most prudent to wait a while for them, and to postpone the final decision to July 1. but that this might occasion as little delay as possible a committee was appointed to prepare a declaration of independence. The commee were J. Adams, Dr. Franklin, Roger Sherman, Robert R. Livingston & myself. Committees were also appointed at the same time to prepare a plan of confederation for the colonies, and to state the terms proper to be proposed for foreign alliance. The committee for drawing the declaration of Independence desired me to do it. It was accordingly done, and being approved by them, I reported it to the house on Friday the 28th of June when it was read and ordered to lie on the table. On Monday, the 1st of July the house resolved itself into a commee of the whole & resumed the consideration of the original motion made by the delegates of Virginia, which being again debated through the day, was carried in the affirmative by the votes of N. Hampshire, Connecticut, Massachusetts, Rhode Island, N. Jersey, Maryland, Virginia, N. Carolina, & Georgia. S. Carolina and Pennsylvania voted against it. Delaware having but two members present, they were divided. The delegates for New York declared they were for it themselves & were assured their constituents were for it, but that their instructions having been drawn near a twelvemonth before, when reconciliation was still the general object, they were enjoined by them to do nothing which should impede that object. They therefore thought themselves not justifiable in voting on either side, and asked leave to withdraw from the question, which was given them. The commee rose & reported their resolution to the house. Mr. Edward Rutledge of S. Carolina then requested the determination might be put off to the next day, as he believed his colleagues, tho' they disapproved of the resolution, would then join in it for the sake of unanimity. The ultimate question whether the house would agree to the resolution of the committee was accordingly postponed to the next day, when it was again moved and S. Carolina concurred in voting for it. In the meantime a third member had come post from the Delaware counties and turned the vote of that colony in favour of the resolution. Members of a different sentiment attending that morning from Pennsylvania also, their vote was changed, so that the whole 12 colonies who were authorized to vote at all, gave their voices for it; and within a few days, the convention of N. York approved of it and thus supplied the void occasioned by the withdrawing of her delegates from the vote.

Congress proceeded the same day to consider the declaration of Independence which had been reported & lain on the table the Friday preceding, and on Monday referred to a commee of the whole. The pusillanimous idea that we had friends in England worth keeping terms with, still haunted the minds of many. For this reason those passages which conveyed censures on the people of England were struck out, lest they should give them offence. The clause too, reprobating the enslaving the inhabitants of Africa, was struck out in complaisance to South Carolina and Georgia, who

had never attempted to restrain the importation of slaves, and who on the contrary still wished to continue it. Our northern brethren also I believe felt a little tender under those censures; for tho' their people have very few slaves themselves yet they had been pretty considerable carriers of them to others. The debates having taken up the greater parts of the 2d 3d & 4th days of July were, in the evening of the last, closed the declaration was reported by the commee, agreed to by the house and signed by every member present except Mr. Dickinson.

The finished Declaration, with its majestic force and solemn dignity, was an expression by Jefferson of the deepest yearnings and ideals of the inarticulate masses, written in words so simple that no man could fail to understand them:

When in the Course of human events, it becomes necessary for one people to dissolve the political bands which have connected them with another, and to assume among the powers of the earth, the separate and equal station to which the Laws of Nature and of Nature's God entitle them, a decent respect to the opinions of mankind requires that they should declare the causes which impel them to the separation. We hold these truths to be self-evident, that all men are created equal, that they are endowed by their Creator with certain unalienable Rights, that among these are Life, Liberty and the pursuit of Happiness. That to secure these rights, Governments are instituted among Men, deriving their just powers from the consent of the governed, That whenever any Form of Government becomes destructive of these ends, it is the Right of the People to alter or to abolish it, and to institute new Government, laying its foundation on such principles and organizing its powers in such form, as to them shall seem most likely to effect their Safety and Happiness. Prudence, indeed, will dictate that Governments long established should not be changed for light and transient causes; and accordingly all experience hath shewn, that mankind are more disposed to suffer, while evils are sufferable, than to right themselves by abolishing the forms to which they are accustomed. But when a long train of abuses and usurpations, pursuing invariably the same Object evinces a design to reduce them under absolute Despotism, it is their right, it is their duty, to throw off such Government, and to provide new Guards for their future security. Such has been the patient sufferance of these Colonies; and such is now the necessity which constrains them to alter their former Systems of Government.

There follows a lengthy, impressive recital by Jefferson of George III's "repeated injuries and usurpations," and he then concludes:

In every stage of these Oppressions We have Petitioned for Redress in the most humble terms: Our repeated Petitions have been answered only by repeated injury. A Prince, whose character is thus marked by every act which may define a Tyrant, is unfit to be the ruler of a free people. Nor have We been wanting in attentions to our Brittish brethren. We have warned them from time to time of attempts by their legislature to extend an unwarrantable jurisdiction over us. We have reminded them of the circumstances of our emigration and settlement here. We have appealed to their native justice and magnanimity, and we have conjured them by the ties of our common kindred to disavow these usurpations, which, would inevitably interrupt our connections and correspondence. They too have been deaf to the voice of justice and of consanguinity. We must, therefore, acquiesce in the necessity, which denounces our Separation, and hold them, as we hold the rest of mankind, Enemies in War, in Peace Friends.

Jefferson's writing table, Independence Hall.

John Hancock's place when he served as president of the Second Continental Congress.

We, therefore, the Representatives of the united States of America, in General Congress, Assembled, appealing to the Supreme Judge of the world for the rectitude of our intentions, do, in the Name, and by Authority of the good People of these Colonies, solemnly publish and declare, That these United Colonies are, and of Right ought to be Free and Independent States; that they are Absolved from all Allegiance to the British Crown, and that all political connection between them and the State of Great Britain, is and ought to be totally dissolved; and that as Free and Independent States, they have full Power to levy War, conclude Peace, contract Alliances, establish Commerce, and to do all other Acts and Things which Independent States may of right do. And for the support of this Declaration, with a firm reliance on the protection of divine Providence, we mutually pledge to each other our Lives, our Fortunes and our sacred Honor.

Having resolved upon independence, Congress took up debate on Jefferson's form of the Declaration. During the overhauling of the text and criticism of the punctuation, debate became so heated at times that Jefferson was reported to have winced. But the young author of thirty-three years remained silent, too modest or too proud to defend his own work. John Adams, probably one of the best debaters in Congress, was the chief protagonist for Jefferson's draft during these heated discussions, and Jefferson never failed in later years to testify to Adams' contribution during those memorable days. The debate continued for three days, with the prospect of being interminable and fruitless, during which time Congress made eighteen suppressions (including Jefferson's denunciation of slavery), six trifling additions, and ten alterations. The Declaration was finally adopted, four members voting against it and New York withholding its vote. It was signed at once by John Hancock, the president of Congress, and Charleston Thomson, the secretary. The remaining signatures on the engrossed copy were affixed on August 2, 1776, with the result that of the fifty-six signers, seven were not members of Congress when it passed.

Writing many years later, possibly in a moment of vanity though certainly without any attempt at denigration, John Adams at the age of eighty-seven was prompted on August 22, 1822, by a letter from the wily Timothy Pickering about the Declaration to reply: "As you justly observe there is not an idea in it but what had been hackneyed in Congress for two years before. The substance of it is contained in the declaration of rights, and the violation of those rights, in the Journals of Congress in 1774. Indeed, the essence of it is contained in a pamphlet, voted and printed by the town of Boston, before the first Congress met, composed by James Otis, as I suppose in one of his lucid intervals, and pruned and polished by Samuel Adams."

On seeing these insinuations in print, Jefferson wrote a letter of admirable restraint and good sense to Madison under the date of August 30, 1823:

Pickering's observations, and Mr. Adams' in addition, 'that it contained no new ideas, that it is a common-place compilation, its sentiments hacknied in Congress for two years before, and its essence contained in Otis' pamphlet,' may all be true. Of that I am not to be the judge. Richard Henry Lee charged it as copied from Locke's treatise on government. Otis' pamphlet I never saw, and whether I had gathered my ideas from reading or reflection I do not know. I know only that I turned to neither book nor pamphlet while writing it. I did not consider it as any part of my charge to invent new ideas altogether, and to offer no sentiment which had ever been expressed before. Had Mr. Adams been so restrained, Con-

gress would have lost the benefit of his bold and impressive advocations of the rights of Revolution. For no man's confident and fervid addresses, more than Mr. Adams', encouraged and supported us through the difficulties surrounding us, which, like the ceaseless action of gravity, weighed on us by night and by day. Yet, on the same ground we may ask, what of these elevated thoughts was new, or can be affirmed never before to have entered the conceptions of man?

Whether, also, the sentiments of Independence, and the reasons for declaring it, which make so great a portion of the instrument, had been hackneyed in Congress for two years before the 4th of July, '76, or this dictum also of Mr. Adams be another slip of memory, let history say. This, however, I will say for Mr. Adams, that he supported the Declaration with zeal and ability, fighting fearlessly for every word of it.

As late as May 8, 1825, within a little more than a year of his death, he declared with his characteristic modesty in a letter to Henry Lee that there was nothing strikingly new or ingenious in the Declaration; in writing it, rather, his intention was

not to find out new principles, or new arguments, never before thought of, not merely to say things which had never been said before; but to place before mankind the common sense of the subject, in terms so plain and firm as to command their assent, and to justify ourselves in the independent stand we are compelled to take. Neither aiming at originality of principle or sentiment, nor yet copied from any particular and previous writing, it was intended to be an expression of the American mind, and to give to that expression the proper tone and spirit called for by the occasion.

CHAPTER IV

POLITICAL ARCHITECT
OF THE COMMONWEALTH
OF VIRGINIA (1776-1779)

The debate on independence and adoption of the Declaration had been Jefferson's immortal hour; his reputation had spread throughout the colonies after the completion of his great work. During these hectic summer days in Philadelphia when widespread public attention was focused on him, he quietly but earnestly observed political developments back home in Virginia with increasing unease and annoyance. From the moment he heard that Virginia was framing a new form of government he was deeply disturbed: he passionately believed in the democratic philosophy of the Declaration, and as a result stoutly challenged the right of the Virginia Convention, elected to wage war, to undertake the making of a constitution without a direct mandate from the people. Jefferson, after all, had been responsible for the resolution of the Continental Congress recommending that "a full and free representation of the people" in such a convention should be assured by the election of delegates for that specific purpose. His recommendation was ignored.

When he hinted repeatedly in his correspondence to influential friends in Williamsburg that he wished to be recalled in order to participate in the work at hand, he was met with a conspiracy of silence. His work in Con-

gress did not appease his fundamental concern over the rigid, entrenched power of the old ruling oligarchic group—this self-perpetuating Tidewater aristocracy—at home. To Jefferson a change in systems in local legislatures was infinitely more important than simply a change in government. Absent from the seat of power at home, he increasingly resented his enforced presence in Philadelphia.

Our delegation had been renewed for the ensuing year commencing Aug. 11. but the new government was now organized, a meeting of the legislature was to be held in Oct. and I had been elected a member by my county. I knew that our legislation under the regal government had many very vicious points which urgently required reformation, and I thought I could be of more use in forwarding that work. I therefore retired from my seat in Congress on the 2d. of Sep. resigned it, and took my place in the legislature of my state, on the 7th. of October.

When the Legislative Assembly convened in Williamsburg on October 7, 1776, Jefferson was there to take his seat. As the first order of business the perennial Edmund Pendleton was elected speaker and Benjamin Harrison selected to fill Jefferson's vacant position in Congress. Jefferson entered at once upon a labor of reform that was to prove the greatest work of his life.

On the 11th. I moved for leave to bring in a bill for the establishment of courts of justice, the organization of which was of importance; I drew the bill it was approved by the commee, reported and passed after going thro' it's due course.

The next day he brought in a much more controversial measure, the bill to abolish entails, which boldly struck a deadly blow at the old landed hereditary aristocracy of Virginia to which he belonged. He had turned upon his own class.

On the 12th. I obtained leave to bring in a bill declaring tenants in tail to hold their lands in fee simple. In the earlier times of the colony when lands were to be obtained for little or nothing, some provident individuals procured large grants, and, desirous of founding great families for themselves, settled them on their descendants in fee-tail. . . . To annul this privilege, and instead of an aristocracy of wealth, of more harm and danger, than benefit, to society, to make an opening for the aristocracy of virtue and talent, which nature has wisely provided for the direction of the interests of society, & scattered with equal hand through all it's conditions, was deemed essential to a well ordered republic. To effect it no violence was necessary, no deprivation of natural right, but rather an enlargement of it by a repeal of the law. For this would authorize the present holder to divide the property among his children equally, as his affections were divided; and would place them, by natural generation on the level of their fellow citizens. But this re-

peal was strongly opposed by Mr. Pendleton, who was zealously attached to ancient establishments; and who, taken all in all, was the ablest man in debate I have ever met with. . . . Finding that the general principles of entails could not be maintained, he took his stand on an amendment which he proposed, instead of an absolute abolition, to permit the tenant in tail to convey in fee simple, if he chose it: and he was within a few votes of saving so much of the old law. But the bill passed finally for entire abolition.

The second bill proposed by Jefferson on that notable day of October 12, 1776, was for a general revision and codification of the laws of Virginia. The bill to accomplish this large purpose was passed later that month. A strong committee comprising some of the best minds to be found in Virginia was appointed to execute the work with Jefferson as chairman. They worked hard at their task from early in 1777:

We had in this work brought so much of the Common law as it was thought necessary to alter, all the British statutes from Magna Charta to the present day, and all the laws of Virginia, from the establishment of our legislature, in the 4th. Jac. 1. to the present time, which we thought should be retained, within the compass of 126 bills, making a printed folio of 90 pages only. Some bills were taken out occasionally, from time to time, and passed; but the main body of the work was not entered on by the legislature until after the general peace, in 1785. when by the unwearied exertions of Mr. Madison, in opposition to the endless quibbles, chicaneries, perversions, vexations and delays of lawyers and demi-lawyers, most of the bills were passed by the legislature, with little alteration.

The problem of slavery with its bitter material and moral defects was a painful abrasive on Jefferson's conscience for his entire life. He was never to conceal his attitude toward slavery, never to miss an opportunity to attempt the writing of his conviction into law.

The bill on the subject of slaves was a mere digest of the existing laws respecting them, without any intimation of a plan for a future & general emancipation. It was thought better that this should be kept back, and attempted only by way of amendment whenever the bill should be brought on. The principles of the amendment however were agreed on, that is to say, the freedom of all born after a certain day, and deportation at a proper age. But it was found that the public mind would not yet bear the proposition, nor will it bear it even at this day. Yet the day is not distant when it must bear and adopt it, or worse will follow. Nothing is more certainly written in the book of fate than that these people are to be free. Nor is it less certain that the two races, equally free, cannot live in the same government. Nature, habit, opinion has drawn indelible lines of distinction between them. It is still in our power to direct the process of emancipation and deportation peaceably and in such slow degree as that the evil will wear off insensibly, and their place be pari passu filled up by free white laborers. If on the contrary it is left to force itself on, human nature must shudder at the prospect held up.

The two great bills which Jefferson drafted for incorporation into the fundamental law of Virginia were the Bill for Establishing Religious Freedom and the Bill for the more General Diffusion of Knowledge. The first, which ranked in importance in Jefferson's opinion with the Declaration of Independence, became law after an epic struggle; the second, one of his dreams, never achieved success, probably because he had overestimated the intelligence of the Assembly.

In expounding his theory and practice of absolute religious freedom and universal and unfettered education, he erected equally supporting twin pillars in the temple of liberty as he pictured it. His complete faith in popular government and in the processes of democratic institutions presupposed a rigid separation of Church and State and a firmly supported system of popular education for the masses. He made clear in drafting these religious and educational measures that democracy can survive only when all men are protected in their civil rights against religious intolerance and persecution, and when all men—independent of wealth, birth, or other accidental circumstances, and in spite of the inequality of their conditions—are given an equal opportunity of an education. With the optimistic ardor characteristic of the Enlightenment, Jefferson was a profound believer in the liberating influence of knowledge. He was, at the same time, increasingly skeptical of revealed religion and expressed disbelief in all clerical establishments and their hierarchical pretensions. So it was in these pronouncements that Jefferson spelled out his deepest and most steadfast convictions concerning the fundamental nature of the relations between man and the state; it was here that he forcefully extended his democratic thesis to its fullest implication.

The provisions for the Bill for the more General Diffusion of Knowledge were most extraordinary for the time, for, with the concepts set forth there, Jefferson was laying the foundations for a system of free and universal public education. To Jefferson it was perfectly clear that popular government could not thrive in ignorance, and therefore that popular edu-

cation could not be neglected in a free society. But in his theory of education, he did not imply that all, regardless of fitness and talent, were entitled to complete schooling from primary through college levels. Education to him constituted a type of selective or pyramidal hierarchy, broad at the base and tapering at the top, where a child of genius would be given an opportunity to develop his native qualities. He explained later in his Autobiography *what he tried to do and why he thought he failed:*

We thought, that on this subject a systematical plan of general education should be proposed, and I was requested to undertake it. I accordingly prepared three bills for the Revisal, proposing three distinct grades of education, reaching all classes. 1. Elementary schools for all children generally, rich and poor. 2. Colleges for a middle degree of instruction, calculated for the common purposes of life, and such as would be desirable for all who were in easy circumstances. And 3d. an ultimate grade for teaching the sciences generally, & in their highest degree. The first bill proposed to lay off every county into Hundreds or Wards, of a proper size and population for a school, in which reading, writing, and common arithmetic should be taught; and that the whole state should be divided into 24 districts, in each of which should be a school for classical learning, grammar, geography, and the higher branches of numerical arithmetic. . . . One provision of the bill was that the expenses of these schools should be borne by the inhabitants of the county, every one in proportion to his general tax-rate. This would throw on wealth the education of the poor; and the justices, being generally of the more wealthy class, were unwilling to incur that burthen, and I believe it was not suffered to commence in a single county.

In Jefferson's mind religion was a private affair: the relation of a man to his God was an affair of the individual conscience in which neither the state nor the established church had a right to intervene. It was inevitable that this self-perpetuating oligarchy of the Church roused him to battle; for a long time he had thought deeply and read extensively on the subject.

The bill for establishing religious freedom, the principles of which had, to a certain degree, been enacted before, I had drawn in all the latitude of reason & right. It still met with opposition; but, with some mutilations in the preamble, it was finally passed; and a singular proposition proved that it's protection of opinion was meant to be universal. Where the preamble declares that coercion is a departure from the plan of the holy author of our religion, an amendment was proposed, by inserting the word "Jesus Christ," so that it should read "a departure from the plan of Jesus Christ, the holy author of our religion" the insertion was rejected by a great majority, in proof that they meant to comprehend, within the mantle of it's protection, the Jew and the Gentile, the Christian and Mahometan, the Hindoo, and infidel of every denomination.

In an atmosphere tense with feeling, when passions and arguments reached white heat over questions of religion in the Assembly, Jefferson remained diligently hard at work drafting some of the noblest utterances ever pronounced on this delicate and controversial subject. In his preamble to the bill he laid down a sweeping affirmation of human rights and religious freedom:

Well aware that the opinions and belief of men depend not on their own will, but follow involuntarily the evidence proposed to their minds; that Almighty God hath created the mind free, and manifested his supreme will that free it shall remain by making it altogether insusceptible of restraint; that all attempts to influence it by temporal punishments, or burthens, or by civil incapacitations, tend only to beget habits of hypocrisy and meanness, and are a departure from the plan of the holy author of our religion. . . . That to compel a man to furnish contributions of money for the propagation of opinions which he disbelieves and abhors, is sinful and tyrannical; that even the forcing him to support this or that teacher of his own religious persuasion, is depriving him of the comfortable liberty of giving his contributions to the particular pastor whose morals he would make his pattern . . . that our civil rights have no dependence on our religious opinions, any more than our opinions of physics or geometry; and therefore the proscribing any citizen as unworthy the public confidence by laying upon him an incapacity of being called to offices of trust or emolument, unless he profess or renounce this or that religious opinion, is depriving him injudiciously of those privileges and advantages to which, in common with his fellow-citizens, he has a natural right . . . that the opinions of men are not the object of civil government, nor under its jurisdiction . . . that truth is great and will prevail if left to herself; that she is the proper and sufficient antagonist to error, and has nothing to fear from the conflict unless by human interposition disarmed of her natural weapons, free argument and debate. . .

Having carefully prepared the philosophical foundations and implications of his argument, Jefferson progressed through the logic of his fundamental assertions in a sustained poetic cadence; he sought to create an unbreachable wall of separation between Church and State and make religious opinions forever private and free from political intrusion. In a ringing declaration of positive law, as well as an exquisite phrasing of lofty principles, he concluded:

We the General Assembly of Virginia do enact that no man shall be compelled to frequent or support any religious worship, place or ministry whatsoever, nor shall be enforced, restrained, molested, or burthened in his body or goods, or shall otherwise suffer, on account of his religious opinions or belief; but that all men shall be free to profess, and by argument to maintain, their opinions in matters of religion, and that the same shall in no wise diminish, enlarge, or affect their civil capacities.

And though we know well that this Assembly, elected by the people for the ordinary purposes of legislation only, have no power to restrain the acts of succeeding Assemblies, constituted with powers equal to our own, and that therefore to declare this act irrevocable would be of no effect in law; yet we are free to declare, and do declare, that the rights hereby asserted, are of the natural rights of mankind, and that if any act shall be hereafter passed to repeal the present or to narrow its operation, such act will be an infringement of natural right.

This bill and its author aroused a storm of antagonism in the Assembly; the opposition savagely attacked sections of the preamble and succeeded in making certain deletions from it. After ten years of persistent struggle on the part of Jefferson's close friends, his bill for religious freedom finally passed in 1786. He was serving on a diplomatic mission in France at the time. The young James Madison reported triumphantly to him the electrifying news that the bill had finally become the law of the land: this was the first law ever passed by a popular assembly giving and guaranteeing perfect freedom of conscience to all citizens.

Although Jefferson's comprehensive program was never fully realized, he lived to see his noble dream become a nearly complete reality as his successive reform bills eventually passed, even if in an altered and compromised state. The ideal form of government he had in mind might be best described as a democracy, but he did not use the word himself; years later when he made his final assessment of these bills in his Autobiography, *he spoke only of "a government truly republican."*

I considered 4 of these bills, passed or reported, as forming a system by which every fibre would be eradicated of antient or future aristocracy; and a foundation laid for a government truly republican. The repeal of the laws of entail would prevent the accumulation and perpetuation of wealth in select families, and preserve the soil of the country from being daily more & more absorbed in Mortmain. The abolition of primogeniture, and equal partition of inheritances removed the feudal and unnatural distinctions which made one member of every family rich, and all the rest poor, substituting equal partition, the best of all Agrarian laws. The restoration of the rights of conscience relieved the people from taxation for the support of a religion not theirs; for the establishment was truly of the religion of the rich, the dissenting sects being entirely composed of the less wealthy people; and these, by the bill for a general education, would be qualified to understand their rights, to maintain them, and to exercise with intelligence their parts in self-government: and all this would be effected without the violation of a single natural right of any one individual citizen.

CHAPTER V

WAR GOVERNOR
OF VIRGINIA
(1779-1781)

JEFFERSON *was thirty-six years old when, on the first of June, 1779, he was elected governor of Virginia by the Assembly to succeed Patrick Henry, the state's first governor under the new order. Jefferson was a candidate of the liberals or reformers, while his friend from youth, John Page, was put forward by the conservatives. Even though the candidates took no part in electioneering, their supporters canvassed vigorously.*

For several months after taking office Jefferson resided in Williamsburg, occupying the Governor's Palace; early in 1780 the seat of government was moved to Richmond, where the legislators were located more centrally and less exposed to the enemy. On taking office, Jefferson found that the finances of the state were in chaos. It cost money to run a state government and to supply its militia with arms, munitions, and all the requisites of war. There simply was little solid money on hand; public and private finances were disintegrating under the shattering impact of the war emergency and uncontrolled inflation. The people resisted and evaded taxes imposed on them by their state government; to solve the problem the Assembly resorted finally to emitting paper money. Rising prices were met with more money in an ever-spiraling inflation.

It was a losing race and Jefferson knew it as he fumbled with desperate measures to bolster the sagging economy and the general depreciation of currency. From Williamsburg he wrote Richard Henry Lee in June 1779:

It is a cruel thought that when we feel ourselves standing on the firmest ground in every respect, the cursed arts of our secret enemies combining with other causes, should effect, by depreciating our money, what the open arms of a powerful enemy could not. What is to be done? Taxation is become of no account, for it is foreseen that notwithstanding it's increased amount there will still be a greater deficiency than ever. I own I see no assured hope but in peace of a plentiful loan of hard money.

From the moment he took office Jefferson was struggling with the accumulating difficulties of a well-equipped enemy pressing hard on every exposed border, yet nagging, more immediate economic problems rose to plague and absorb much of his energy. As the shadows of economic depression deepened in the fall of 1779, a blight fell upon the crops and threatened the beleaguered state's food supply. In a letter to John Jay, then president of the Continental Congress, he described the crisis:

The various calamities which during the present year have befallen our crops of wheat, have reduced them so very low as to leave us little more than seed for the ensuing year, were it to be solely applied to that purpose. This country is therefore unable to furnish the necessary supplies of flour for the Convention troops, without lessening by so much as should be purchased, the sowing for another crop. . . .

Our trade has never been so distressed since the time of Lord Dunmore as it is at present by a parcel of trifling privateers under the countenance of two or three larger vessels who keep our little naval force from doing any thing. The uniform train of events which during the whole course of this war we are to suppose has rendered it improper that the American fleet or any part of it should ever come to relieve or countenance the trade of certain places, while the same train of events has as uniformly rendered it proper to confine them to the protection of certain other parts of the continent is a lamentable arrangement of fortune for us. The same ill luck has attended us as to the disposition of the prizes taken by our navy, which tho' sometimes taken just off our capes, it has always been expedient to carry elsewhere. A British prize would be a more rare phaenomenon here than a comet, because the one has been seen, but the other never was.

For all the economic turmoil and confusion at home, Jefferson fastened his attention on the ominous movements of the British army to the south. North Carolina had been raided and South Carolina was under heavy attack as the British shifted the main theater of operations to the south. But Jefferson felt he was groping for accurate information in a fog of blind ignorance as a result of an inexcusably defective intelligence network. He wrote to Washington that he was establishing a line of messengers

to remedy this deficiency. The peace-loving governor was unprepared psychologically to cope with the violent reality of war.

The normal military resources of the state had been exhausted in responding to the urgent calls from Congress and Washington; the state was helpless, Jefferson feared, to resist an invasion.

There is really nothing to oppose the progress of the enemy Northward but the cautious principles of the military art. North Caroline is without arms. We do not abound. Those we have are freely imparted to them, but such is the state of their resources that they have not yet been able to move a single musket from this state to theirs. All the waggons we can collect have been furnished to the Marquis de Kalb, and are assembling for the march of 2500 militia under Genl. Stevens of Culpeper who will move on the 19th. inst. I have written to Congress to hasten supplies of arms and military stores for the Southern states, and particularly to aid us with Cartridge paper and Cartridge boxes, the want of which articles, small as they are, renders our stores useless. The want of money cramps every effort.

Throughout these dark years Jefferson, like Washington, remained a steadfast nationalist in his broad view of the raging conflict, always thinking in terms of the whole. He tried hard to respond to all the desperate calls that came in from north and south for help. Virginia's militia, considering the vast size to be defended, was small; worse still, it was inexperienced; and worst of all, it was wretchedly supplied with arms and munitions.

The steady march of enemy northward, although impeded, could not be checked. In October a British fleet with three thousand British regulars under General Leslie aboard

Tea room at the Governor's Palace, Williamsburg.

sailed into Hampton Roads. The invaders expected to join forces with Cornwallis, whom they expected was advancing toward Virginia. Jefferson made every possible effort to collect an adequate body of men to oppose the enemy, at the same time he was attempting to cope with a hideous lack of arms. He warned Benjamin Harrison, then speaker of the House, in December 1780:

I think it my duty also to mention to the General Assembly that I have received information from [Baron von Steuben] that a very considerable proportion of the new Levies raised under an act of the last session of Assembly and now at Chesterfield are totally unfit for service, where much fatigue and hardship is to be endured, being old men, boys or decrepid: and for this reason he means to decline continuing them in Continental service and return them to the State.

When Leslie learned Cornwallis was retreating, not advancing in the south, he took ship and sailed away.

Early in January 1781 the thunderbolt

finally struck Virginia. A large, powerful British fleet sailed out of New York under the command of the American traitor Benedict Arnold, entered the James River, and launched a full-scale invasion of Virginia. There was some initial confusion as to just how far up the river the British intended to penetrate, but it did not take long to ascertain that the primary objective of the British expedition was Richmond and the destruction of supplies and the disruption of government there. Overnight the town was thrown into feverish activity and confused disarray; members of the Assembly scurried for cover and scattered to their counties to supervise the raising of militia forces. Jefferson hurriedly wrote to the county lieutenants of twenty-one counties on January 2nd requesting them immediately to call forth "one fourth of your Militia":

That there may not be a moments delay, let them come in detached parcels as they can be collected, every man who has arms bringing them.

The county lieutenants of counties located near Richmond were ordered

to repair immediately to Richmond armed with good Rifles and Accoutrements suitable as far they have them; such of them as have not Rifles will be armed here with Musquets and joined to the Battalions of Musquetry. Those who bring Rifles will be formed into a separate Corps. Much will depend on the proper Choice of Officers.

In a daring, well-timed exploit, Arnold marched with lightning speed through the enemy, where he met only token resistance, and marched into Richmond in triumph. Jefferson reported to Washington on January 10th:

They marched from Westover at 2 o Clock in the afternoon of the 4th. and entered Richmond at 1 o Clock in the afternoon of the 5th. A regiment of infantry and about 30 horse continued on without halting to the Foundery. They burnt that, the boring mill the magazine and two other houses, and proceeded to Westham, but nothing being in their power there they retired to Richmond. The next morning they burnt some buildings of public and some of private property, with what Stores remained in them, destroyed a great quantity of private Stores and about 12 o Clock retired towards Westover where they encamped within the neck the next day. . . . At the Foundery we lost the greater part of the papers belonging to the auditors office, and of the books and papers of the Council office. About 5 or 6 tons as we conjecture of powder was thrown into the canal of which there will be a considerable saving by remanufacturing it. The roof of the foundery was burnt but the Stacks of Chimnies and furnaces not at all injured. The boring mill was consumed. Within less than 48 hours from the time of their landing and 19 from our knowing their destination they had penetrated 33 miles, done the whole injury and retired.

Humiliation at the hands of Arnold turned to bitter wrath, and, writing to General Muhlenburg in late January 1781, Jefferson suggested a plot, offering a handsome reward, to capture the traitor and bring him to justice.

Acquainted as you are with the treasons of Arnold, I need say nothing for your information, or to give you a proper sentiment of them. You will readily suppose that it is above all things desireable to drag him from those under whose wing he is now sheltered. . . . Having peculiar confidence in the men from the Western side of the mountains, I meant as soon as they should come down to get the enterprize proposed to a chosen number of them, such whose courage and whose fidelity would be above all doubt. Your perfect knowlege of those men personally, and my confidence in your discretion, induce me to ask you to pick from among them proper characters, in such number as you think best, to reveal to them our desire, and engage them [to] undertake to seize and bring off this greatest of all traitors. . . . I will undertake if they are succesful in bringing him off alive, that they shall receive five thousand guineas reward among them, and to men formed for such an enterprize it must be a great incitement to know that their names will be recorded with glory in history.

There followed an interlude of inactivity for several months before the British were on the march again. In the midst of these dark events of war, personal tragedy was added to Jefferson's troubles when his baby daughter died on April 19th. By May the British forces under Phillips and the hated Arnold were once again on the move and sailed up the James River. They entered Williamsburg and threatened Richmond; alarm and fear gripped Virginia as the greater part of the state was helpless before a marauding enemy army. From late April into May, during the days of greatest peril when the dark clouds of invasion and war hung over the state, the business of civil government was abdicated and came to a standstill. Elected officials disappeared from the scene; even though Jefferson called daily sessions of the Council, no quorum could be had. With the real crisis looming large in early May and with Jefferson clamoring to Congress for arms and reinforcements from the trained troops in the north, he reported to Washington on a recent action of the militia, who, he found,

occasionally performed with surprising bravery in the face of so many crippling handicaps.

The Enemy after leaving Williamsburg came directly up James River and landed at City point being the point of Land on the Southern Side of the Confluence of Appomattox and James Rivers; they marched up to Petersburg where they were received by Major General Baron Steuben with a Body of Militia somewhat under 1000, who 'tho the Enemy were 2300 strong disputed the Ground very handsomely two Hours during which time the Enemy gained one mile only and that by inches. Our Troops were then ordered to retire over a Bridge which they did in perfect good Order. Our Loss was between sixty and seventy killed wounded and taken: the Enemy's is unknown but from Circumstances of Probability it must have been equal to ours; for their own Honour they must confess this, as they broke twice and run like Sheep till supported by fresh Troops. An Inferiority of Number obliged our Force to withdraw about 12 Miles upwards, till more Militia should be assembled. . . .

Ill armed and untried Militia who never before saw the Face of an Enemy have at times during this War given Occasion of Exultation to our Enemies, but they afforded us while at Warwick a little Satisfaction in the same way.

By late May the British were on the march again in full force in conjunction with Lord Cornwallis' army, which had finally come up from the south, and ravaged the state with fire and sword. The state government was in a shambles: the Council assembled a bare quorum on May 10th, approved a few emergency measures, adjourned, and scattered in fright; the Assembly decided Richmond was too exposed to the enemy, selected Charlottesville as a safer place to meet, met on May 24th, and in panic voted Jefferson unlimited powers, and, except for two other members besides Jefferson, vanished into limbo until the middle of June. In the midst of the most serious invasion of the war, Jefferson with a heavy heart wrote Washington in late May, informing him of the progress of the enemy and making one last desperate appeal to him to return and personally rally the scattered, disheartened, beaten colonial forces and save the state they both loved.

Jefferson's second term in the gubernatorial office ended abruptly and ingloriously on June 1, 1781. He was eligible for reelection for a third term, but he was determined to resign. He felt a mingled sense of helplessness and bitterness—and a genuine sense of release— when he handed in his resignation to bring to a close his two years of tenure in office. In the last dark days of his regime, with the Continental army in full retreat, the Virginia legis-

lators suffered a crisis of faith and courage, and fell back on the last recourse of the timid: the creation of a dictatorship. In early June following Jefferson's resignation and hasty departure for Monticello, the legislature neglected to choose a successor and Virginia was without a governor for twelve days. A party arose in the crisis advocating a dictator. The very thought filled Jefferson with vehemence and rage; writing within two years of the event in his Notes on Virginia, *he expressed his intense feelings about this outrageous plan and set down for his countrymen an immortal statement on the latent dangers of despotism in a free society.*

In December 1776, our circumstances being much distressed, it was proposed in the house of delegates to create a *dictator*, invested with every power legislative, executive and judiciary, civil and military, of life and of death, over our persons and over our proper-

Point of Forks at the confluence of the Rivanna and James Rivers.

ties: and in June 1781, again under calamity, the same proposition was repeated, and wanted a few votes only of being passed. . . . The very thought alone was treason against the people; was treason against mankind in general; as rivetting for ever the chains which bow down their necks, by giving to their oppressors a proof, which they would have trumpeted through the universe, of the imbecility of republican government, in times of pressing danger, to shield them from harm.

When Jefferson retired to his secluded mountain of Monticello in June 1781, he may have thought he was finished with troubles and humiliations, but fate had a few more in store for him.

It has been said before that the legislature was driven from Charlottesville, by an incursion of the enemy's cavalry. Since the adjournment from Richmond, their force in this country had been greatly augmented by reinforcements under Ld. Cornwallis and General Phillips; and they had advanced up into the country as far as Elk island, and the Fork of James river. Learning that the legislature was in session at Charlottesville, they detached Colo. Tarleton with his legion of horse to surprise them. As he was passing through Louisa on the evening of the 3d. of June, he was observed by a Mr. Jouett, who suspecting the object, set out immediately for Charlottesville, and knowing the by-ways of the neighborhood, passed the enemy's encampment, rode all night, and before sun-rise of the 4th. called at Monticello with notice of what he had seen, and passed on to Charlottesville to notify the members of the legislature. The Speakers of the two houses, and some other members were lodging with us. I ordered a carriage to be ready to carry off my family; we breakfasted

at leisure with our guests, and after breakfast they had gone to Charlottesville; when a neighbor rode up full speed to inform me that a troop of horse was then ascending the hill to the house. I instantly sent off my family, and, after a short delay for some pressing arrangements, I mounted my horse, and knowing that in the public road I should be liable to fall in with the enemy, I went thro' the woods, and joined my family at the house of a friend where we dined.

In 1788 when Dr. William Gordon asked Jefferson for details of his suffering at the hands of Tarleton, he wrote:

I did not suffer by [Tarleton]. On the contrary he behaved very genteelly with me. On his approach to Charlottesville which is within 3. miles of my house at Monticello, he dispatched a troop of his horse under Capt. Mc.leod with the double object of taking me prisoner with the two Speakers of the Senate and Delegates who then lodged with me, and remaining there in vedette, my house commanding a view of 10. or 12 counties round about. He gave strict orders to Capt. Mc.leod to suffer nothing to be injured. . . . It was early in June 1781. Lord Cornwallis then proceeded to the point of fork, and encamped his army from thence all along the main James river to a seat of mine called Elkhill, opposite to Elk island and a little below the mouth of the Byrd creek. (You will see all these places exactly laid down in the map annexed to my Notes on Virginia printed by Stockdale.) He remained in this position ten days, his own head quarters being in my house at that place. I had had time to remove most of the effects out of the house. He destroyed all my growing crops of corn and tobacco, he burned all my barns containing the same articles of the last year, having first taken what corn he wanted, he used, as was to be expected, all my stocks of cattle, sheep, and hogs for the sustenance of his army, and carried off all the horses capable of service: of those too young for service he cut the throats, and he burnt all the fences on the plantation, so as to leave it an absolute waste. He carried off also about 30. slaves: had this been to give them freedom he would have done right, but it was to consign them to inevitable death from the small pox and putrid fever then raging in his camp. This I knew afterwards to have been the fate of 27. of them. I never had news of the remaining three, but presume they shared the same fate. When I say that Lord Cornwallis did all this, I do not mean that he carried about the torch in his own hands, but that it was all done under his eye, the situation of the house, in which he was, commanding a view of every part of the plantation, so that he must have seen every fire. I relate these things on my own knowlege in a great degree, as I was on the ground soon after he left it. He treated the rest of the neighborhood somewhat in the same stile, but not with that spirit of total extermination with which he seemed to rage over my possessions. Wherever he went, the dwelling houses were plundered of every thing which could be carried off. Lord Cornwallis's character in England would forbid the belief that he shared in the plunder. But that his table was served with the plate thus pillaged from private houses can be proved by many hundred eye witnesses. From an estimate I made at that time on the best information I could collect, I supposed the state of Virginia lost under Ld. Cornwallis's hands that year about 30,000 slaves, and that of these about 27,000 died of the small pox and camp fever, and the rest were partly sent to the West Indies and exchanged for rum, sugar, coffee and fruits, and partly sent to New York, from whence they went at the peace either to Nova Scotia, or England. From this last place I believe they have been lately sent to Africa. History will never relate the horrors committed by the British army in the *Southern* states of America.

Misfortunes continued to mount upon Jefferson's weary body and spirit. When the members of the Assembly reconstituted themselves across the Blue Ridge Mountains in Staunton following their narrow brush with Tarleton's troops, they met in bitterness and defeat; they desperately needed a scapegoat to assume the blame for their deplorable condition. Ugly rumors and angry recriminations were circulating; Jefferson's enemies began to speak of personal cowardice, omissions of duty, and even malfeasance openly, and adoption of an official censure of his conduct in office.

By the time the new Assembly met in December and took up the resolution of inquiry, however, Jefferson's friends rallied, the opposition failed to press its charges, Cornwallis surrendered at Yorktown, and all parties agreed "in the strongest manner, to declare the high opinion which they entertain of Mr. Jefferson's ability, rectitude and integrity, as Chief Magistrate of this Commonwealth; and mean by thus publicly avowing their opinion, to obviate all future, and to remove all former, unmerited censure." Vindicated, Jefferson resigned his seat in the House the same day he had been cleared, and returned to Monticello.

The Marquis de Chastellux, an observant, intelligent Frenchman traveling through Virginia and other states, visited Monticello in the spring of 1782 and has left a sharply etched description of the house and its master:

"This house, of which Mr. Jefferson was the architect, and often the builder, is constructed in an Italian style, and is quite tasteful, although not however without some faults; it

consists of a large square pavilion, into which one enters through two porticoes ornamented with columns. The ground floor consists chiefly of a large and lofty salon, or drawing room, which is to be decorated entirely in the antique style; above the salon is a library of the same form; two small wings, with only a ground floor and attic, are joined to this pavilion, and are intended to communicate with the kitchen, offices, etc. which will form on either side a kind of basement topped by a terrace. My object in giving these details is not to describe the house, but to prove that it resembles none of the others seen in this country;

"Mr. Jefferson is the first American who has consulted the Fine Arts to know how he should shelter himself from the weather."

so that it may be said that Mr. Jefferson is the first American who has consulted the Fine Arts to know how he should shelter himself from the weather. But it is with him alone that I should concern myself.

"Let me then describe to you a man, not yet forty, tall, and with a mild and pleasing countenance, but whose mind and attainments could serve in lieu of all outward graces. . . . A gentle and amiable wife, charming children whose education is his special care, a house to embellish, extensive estates to improve, the arts and sciences to cultivate—these are what remain to Mr. Jefferson, after having played a distinguished role on the stage of the New World, and what he has preferred to the honorable commission of Minister Plenipotentiary in Europe."

"A gentle and amiable wife": how suddenly, how abruptly, how cruelly and alarmingly it all ended in the ultimate tragedy for Jefferson. On September 6, 1782, Martha Wayles Jefferson died. At thirty-nine he was left a grief-stricken widower. After the birth of a daughter, Lucy Elizabeth, on May 8, Mrs. Jefferson's health began to sink rapidly. She had never been a healthy woman, and the strain of her pregnancy and delivery, the care of both her own daughters and the Carr children, the hurried flight from Monticello all had combined to drain her strength. Jefferson stayed close by her side and watched in anguish as her life ebbed; he scarcely left her bedside. His daughter in later years wrote a vivid account of the intensity of his devotion during her final illness and after her death, when he "walked almost incessantly night and day,

only lying down occasionally, when nature was completely exhausted, on a pallet that had been brought in during his long fainting-fit. My aunts remained constantly with him for some weeks—I do not remember how many. When at last he left his room, he rode out, and from that time he was incessantly on horseback, rambling about the mountain, in the least frequented roads, and just as often through the woods. In those melancholy rambles I was his constant companion—a solitary witness to many a burst of grief, the remembrance of which has consecrated particular scenes of that lost home beyond the power of time to obliterate."

The shock to Jefferson was cataclysmic; he withdrew from the world and wrote few letters. The depth of his feeling was expressed in a simple, cryptic entry in his account book: "Sept. 6—my dear wife died this day at 11-45 A.M." This was the first and last time he permitted himself to use an endearing adjective there. He never fully recovered from his despair and distraught frame of mind over her loss—he never used her name on paper again, he never remarried, he carefully destroyed prior to his own death the letters that had passed between them, and he never spoke of the event except by indirection. Martha Jefferson was buried in the little family enclosure on the side of the mountain, in which rested three of her infants. He was not the man to speak of himself and his sorrows, even to his closest friends; about this time, however, he wrote in a small pocket notebook: "There is a time in human suffering when exceeding sorrows are but like snow falling on an iceberg."

CHAPTER VI

APPRENTICESHIP
OF A STATESMAN
(1781–1784)

Following *his retirement as governor in June 1781, when his misfortunes culminated in Tarleton's raid on Monticello and the legislature's move to inquire into his official conduct, Jefferson sought refuge at Poplar Forest, his country retreat some ninety miles from Monticello, where he worked zealously on a manuscript which ultimately appeared under the title of* Notes on the State of Virginia. *Released from the world of war and politics, and during a period of enforced inactivity following a bad fall from his horse, he worked rapidly on the manuscript. In his preface he said the book was "written in Virginia in the year 1781, and somewhat corrected and enlarged in the winter of 1782, in answer to Queries proposed to the Author, by a Foreigner of Distinction, then residing among us." Sometime late in 1780 the secretary of the French legation in America, François, Marquis de Barbé-Marbois, prepared a long series of questions at the request of his government and sent them to those men in the several states most likely to know the answers. On the recommendation of Joseph Jones, a Virginia member of Congress, the set on Virginia was sent to Jefferson. He relished his assignment and set to work immediately with high enthusiasm for this task,*

in spite of the chaotic military state of affairs and the hopelessness of his administration.

⌐ *The* Notes *commenced with a prosaic, matter-of-fact description of the geography of Virginia—its boundaries, rivers, mountains, cascades, and caverns—which he developed and amplified into a luxuriance of supporting material and curious information. He wrote of things that interested him deeply and he wrote from his heart; the* Notes, *even more than his fragmentary* Autobiography, *throw an intimate light on his tastes, curiosities, and political and social opinions. When he came to the rivers of Virginia, and ranged out to the Mississippi, the Ohio, the Missouri, and the Illinois Rivers, he could astound the reader with details: the length of each, the tributaries that feed them, their navigability, the fish. "The Ohio," which he had never seen but of which he had read everything available, "is the most beautiful river on earth. Its current gentle, waters clear, and bosom smooth and unbroken by rocks and rapids, a single instance only excepted." The Mississippi, he added, "will be one of the principal channels of future commerce for the country westward of the Alleghaney"; he likened its floods to those of the Nile. His knowledge of his native Potomac was firsthand; his eloquent description of the passage of the river through the Blue Ridge Mountains was ecstatic and tinged with the sentimentality of romantic poetry.*

The passage of the Patowmac through the Blue ridge is perhaps one of the most stupendous scenes in nature. You stand on a very high point of land. On your right comes up the Shenandoah, having ranged along the foot of the mountain an hundred miles to seek a vent. On your left approaches the Patowmac, in quest of a passage also. In the moment of their junction they rush together against the mountain, rend it asunder, and pass off to the sea. The first glance of this scene hurries our senses into the opinion, that this earth has been created in time, that the mountains were formed first, that the rivers began to flow afterwards, that in this place particularly they have been dammed up by the Blue ridge of mountains, and have formed an ocean which filled the whole valley; that continuing to rise they have at length broken over at this spot, and have torn the mountain down from its summit to its base. The piles of rock on each hand, but particularly on the Shenandoah, the evident marks of their disrupture and avulsion from their beds by the most powerful agents of nature, corroborate the impression. But the distant finishing which nature has given to the picture is of a very different character. It is a true contrast to the fore-ground. It is as placid and delightful, as that is wild and tremendous. For the mountain being cloven asunder, she presents to your eye, through the cleft, a small catch of smooth blue horizon, at an infinite distance in the plain country, inviting you, as it were, from the riot and tumult roaring around, to pass through the breach and participate of the calm below.

From his youth, few natural scenes fasci-

nated him more than the Natural Bridge, in which, as owner of the site, he had a particular pride.

The *Natural bridge*, the most sublime of Nature's works, though not comprehended under the present head, must not be pretermitted. It is on the ascent of a hill, which seems to have been cloven through its length by some great convulsion./ . . . Though the sides of this bridge are provided in some parts with a parapet of fixed rocks, yet few men have resolution to walk to them and look over into the abyss. You involuntarily fall on your hands and feet, creep to the parapet and peep over it. Looking down from this height about a minute, gave me a violent head ach. This painful sensation is relieved by a short, but pleasing view of the Blue ridge along the fissure downwards, and upwards by that of the Short hills, which, with the Purgatory mountain is a divergence from the North ridge; and, descending then to the valley below, the sensation becomes delightful in the extreme. It is impossible for the emotions, arising from the sublime, to be felt beyond what they are here: so beautiful an arch, so elevated, so light, and springing, as it were, up to heaven, the rapture of the Spectator is really indiscribable!

Jefferson was one of the first native-born writers to discover and depict to Europeans the beauty of American natural scenery, and to proclaim with genuine pride that "this scene is worth a voyage across the Atlantic—and is perhaps one of the most stupendous in nature."
With polemic vigor Jefferson protested against the assertion of the great French naturalist, the Count de Buffon, that "the animals common both to the old and new world are smaller in the latter, that those peculiar to the new are in a smaller scale, that those which

have been domesticated in both have degenerated in America." He also took exception to another of Buffon's misconceived assertions: that the American aborigines were as proportionately degenerate to European man as the American mammal was to the European one. He argued that the Indian was brave and enduring, faithful to his friends and affectionate to his children, possessed of a keen sensibility and capable of eloquent oratory.

I may challenge the whole orations of Demosthenes and Cicero, and of any more eminent orator, if Europe has furnished more eminent, to produce a single passage, superior to the speech of Logan, a Mingo chief, to Lord Dunmore, when governor of this state. And, as a testimony of their talents in this line, I beg leave to introduce it, first stating the incidents necessary for understanding it. In the spring of the year 1774, a robbery was committed by some Indians on certain land-adventurers on the river Ohio. The whites in that quarter, according to their custom, undertook to punish this outrage in a summary way. Captain Michael Cresap, and a certain Daniel Great-house, leading on these parties, surprized, at different times, travelling and hunting parties of the Indians, having their women and children with them, and murdered many. Among these were unfortunately the family of Logan, a chief celebrated in peace and war, and long distinguished as the friend of the whites. This unworthy return provoked his vengeance. He accordingly signalized himself in the war which ensued. . . . The Indians were defeated, and sued for peace. Logan however disdained to be seen among the suppliants. But, lest the sincerity of a treaty should be distrusted, from which so distinguished a

Poplar Forest, begun by Jefferson as a retreat in 1806 and completed in 1817, in a majestic stand of tulip poplars.

Peaks of Otter, near Poplar Forest.

chief absented himself, he sent by a messenger the following speech to be delivered to Lord Dunmore.

"I appeal to any white man to say, if ever he entered Logan's cabin hungry, and he gave him not meat; if ever he came cold and naked, and he clothed him not. During the course of the last long and bloody war, Logan remained idle in his cabin, an advocate for peace. Such was my love for the whites, that my country-men pointed as they passed, and said, 'Logan is the friend of white men.' I had even thought to have lived with you, but for the injuries of one man. Col Cresap, the last spring, in cold blood, and unprovoked, murdered all the relations of Logan, not sparing even my women and children. There runs not a drop of my blood in the veins of any living creature. This called on me for revenge. I have sought it: I have killed many: I have fully glutted my vengeance. For my country, I rejoice at the beams of peace. But do not harbour a thought that mine is the joy of fear. Logan never felt fear. He will not turn on his heel to save his life. Who is there to mourn for Logan?—Not one."

Throughout the book Jefferson repeatedly returns to the uniqueness of the American experience, and even tiresomely harps on the difference between the American and European systems of government, principles of economy, and types of civilization.

Those who labour in the earth are the chosen people of God, if ever he had a chosen people, whose breasts he has made his peculiar deposit for substantial and genuine virtue. It is the focus in which he keeps alive that sacred fire, which otherwise might escape from the face of the earth. Corruption of morals in the mass of cultivators is a phænomenon of which no age nor nation has furnished an example. It is the mark set on those, who not looking up to heaven, to their own soil and industry, as does the husbandman, for their subsistance, depend for it on the casualties and caprice of customers. Dependance begets subservience and venality, suffocates the germ of virtue, and prepares fit tools for the designs of ambition. This, the natural progress and consequence of the arts, has sometimes perhaps been retarded by accidental circumstances: but, generally speaking, the proportion which the aggregate of the other classes of citizens bears in any state to that of its husbandmen, is the proportion of its unsound to its healthy parts, and is a good-enough barometer whereby to measure its degree of corruption. While we have land to labour then, let us never wish to see our citizens occupied at a work-bench, or twirling a distaff. Carpenters, masons, smiths, are wanting in husbandry: but, for the general operations of manufacture, let our work-shops remain in Europe. It is better to carry provisions and materials to workmen there, than bring them to the provisions and materials, and with them their manners and principles.

Jefferson was never able to overcome this distrust of large cities, of manufactures, and of industrial workers. His Arcadian vision of an America given completely over to agricultural pursuits, a nation of small cultivators, became a primary article of faith in his political rhetoric. Yet, when he came to write the actual conclusion of the Notes *in his chapter on "Public Revenue and Expences," where he outlines the future policy with foreign nations in times of peace, he formulated an adjusted and modified ideal—an ideal less strident in tone and less nativist in content. He desired for an independent America a real peace, a peace of commercial intercourse with all nations.*

Young as we are, and with such a country before us to fill with people and with happiness, we should point in that direction the whole generative force of nature, wasting none of it in efforts of mutual destruction. It should be our endeavour to cultivate the peace and friendship of every nation, even of that which has injured us most, when we shall have carried our point against her. Our interest will be to throw open the doors of commerce, and to knock off all its shackles, giving perfect freedom to all persons for the vent of whatever they may chuse to bring into our ports, and asking the same in theirs. Never was so much false arithmetic employed on any subject, as that which has been employed to persuade nations that it is their interest to go to war. Were the money which it has cost to gain, at the close of a long war, a little town, or a little territory, the right to cut wood here, or to catch fish there, expended in improving what they already possess, in making roads, opening rivers, building ports, improving the arts, and finding employment for their idle poor, it would render them much stronger, much wealthier and happier. This I hope will be our wisdom.

Such were the Notes on Virginia, *called by William Peden "one of America's first permanent literary and intellectual landmarks," and amazingly the only full-length book Jefferson ever wrote and published during his lifetime.*

On June 6, 1783, his friends maneuvered his appointment as a delegate to Congress, to take office on November 1st. Jefferson spent the summer and early fall at Monticello with the children, his own and those of his sister Martha Carr, and entertained himself drawing up a catalogue of his library. The middle of October he departed for Philadelphia, accompanied by his daughter Martha (whom he called Patsy), arriving on October 29th. The other two daughters were too young to travel, and were left in the care of his sister-in-law, Mrs. Francis Eppes. Congress had adjourned, first to Princeton and finally to Annapolis, in the face of a gang of Continental Army soldiers mutinying over pay. Everything was in chaos. He placed Patsy in the home of the mother of Francis Hopkinson and set out for Annapolis with Madison to catch up with the wandering Congress. There from December 1783 to May 1784 Jefferson worked hard, serving as a member on (and often as chairman of) a number of committees in a sparsely populated Congress.

The education of Patsy remained very much on her father's mind; he had barely settled himself in his new Annapolis lodgings when he sat down and formulated a rigid schedule of studies and activities for the eleven-year-old girl to follow.

The conviction that you would be more improved in the situation I have placed you than if still with me, has solaced me on my parting with you, which my love for you has rendered a difficult thing. The acquirements which I hope you will make under the tutors I have provided for you will render you more worthy of my love, and if they cannot increase it they will prevent it's diminution. Consider the good lady who has taken you under her roof, who has undertaken to see that you perform all your exercises, and to admonish you in all those wanderings from what is right or what is clever to which your inexperience would expose you, consider her I say as your mother, as the only person to whom, since the loss with which heaven has been pleased to afflict you, you can now look up; and that her displeasure

or disapprobation on any occasion will be an immense misfortune which should you be so unhappy as to incur by any unguarded act, think no concession too much to regain her good will. With respect to the distribution of your time the following is what I should approve.

from 8. to 10 o'clock practise music.
from 10. to 1. dance one day and draw another.
from 1. to 2. draw on the day you dance, and write a letter the next day.
from 3. to 4. read French.
from 4. to 5. exercise yourself in music.
from 5. till bedtime read English, write &c.

He explained his system of education to Marbois in Philadelphia, since, as he said in a letter of appreciation, "you were so kind as to undertake of presenting a French tutor to my daughter and for the very friendly dispositions and attentions you flatter me with." Jefferson gave his views on what he considered necessary reading for the fair sex and concluded with a surprisingly cynical view of the intellectual capacities of the Virginia gentry from whom Patsy would in all probability eventually choose a mate.

The plan of reading which I have formed for her is considerably different from what I think would be most proper for her sex in any other country than America. I am obliged in it to extend my views beyond herself, and consider her as possibly at the head of a little family of her own. The chance that in marriage she will draw a blockhead I calculate at about fourteen to one, and of course that the education of her family will probably rest on her own ideas and direction without assistance.

A little later in early December, still waiting

for delinquent members of Congress to arrive, Jefferson found time to reassure his daughter, who had been frightened by gossip interpreting an earthquake as a sign that the world was coming to an end.

I hope you will have good sense enough to disregard those foolish predictions that the world is to be at an end soon. The almighty has never made known to any body at what time he created it, nor will he tell any body when he means to put an end to it, if ever he means to do it. As to preparations for that event, the best way is for you to be always prepared for it. The only way to be so is never to do nor say a bad thing. If ever you are about to say any thing amiss or to do any thing wrong, consider before hand. You will feel something within you which will tell you it is wrong and ought not to be said or done: this is your conscience, and be sure to obey it. Our maker has given us all, this faithful internal Monitor, and if you always obey it, you will always be prepared for the end of the world: or for a much more certain event which is death.

This remarkable man not only planned and critically followed the studies of his young daughters, but throughout their girlhood advised them on their tastes and habits in dress and appearance. In late December 1783 he was again at his desk writing to Patsy:

Some ladies think they may under the privileges of the dishabille be loose and negligent of their dress in the morning. But be you from the moment you rise till you go to bed as cleanly and properly dressed as at the hours of dinner or tea. A lady who has been seen as a sloven or slut in the morning, will never efface the impression she then made with all the dress and pageantry she can afterwards involve herself in.

Jefferson's pre-eminence in the Congress meeting in Annapolis was conceded, for in reputation, past achievements, and ability he loomed conspicuously above his colleagues. When the articles of the peace treaty, with provisions for ending the war and with its recognition of American independence, was signed in Paris and sent to Congress, Jefferson was appointed chairman of a special committee charged with the duty of steering it through to ratification. He submitted the report on the treaty on December 16, 1783, recommending ratification. The plenipotentiaries in Paris had signed the treaty on September 3rd; it contained a clause which made it effective only if

Site of the negotiation of the treaty of commerce and alliance with France, 1778.

ratifications were exchanged between the signatory powers in six months—and this meant actual delivery of the signed document in Europe.

By the end of December only two months of time remained, and still there did not seem to be a sufficient interest among some of the states to send delegates. On December 23rd, according to his Autobiography, Jefferson sent out frantic appeals to the governors of the absent states to hasten their delegations, "stating the receipt of the definitive treaty; that seven States only were in attendance, while nine were necessary to its ratification," with a warning that their absence imperiled the peace. Utterly incredible as it seems, there was no response for weeks from the indifferent governors. The morale of the war-weary country was inexplicably low after the surrender of Cornwallis. Congress itself was given to the most tedious, long-winded debate and haggling over small points in this session; Jefferson has left a vivid account in his Autobiography of this Congress:

Our body was little numerous, but very contentious. Day after day was wasted on the most unimportant questions. My colleague Mercer was one of those afflicted with the morbid rage of debate, of an ardent mind, prompt imagination, and copious flow of words, he heard with impatience any logic which was not his own. Sitting near me on some occasion of a trifling but wordy debate, he asked how I could sit in silence hearing so much false reasoning which a word should refute? I observed to him that to refute indeed was easy, but to silence impossible. That in measures brought forward by myself, I took the laboring oar, as was incumbent on me; but that in general I was willing to listen.

Several members of Jefferson's committee were so alarmed by the shortness of time available that violent arguments ensued, some demanding an unconstitutional ratification on the basis of seven states. Fortunately New Jersey and New Hampshire finally appeared on January 14th and the requisite number of nine states was achieved. The ratification, prepared by Jefferson, was rushed to a vote, duly passed, and Congress relapsed into inertia.

In spite of the interminable talk and debate when no one was exercising much real executive authority, Jefferson realized that the state of the nation required that business somehow be transacted in an orderly fashion. There was the mammoth problem of what was to be done with lands west of the frontier. Virginia generously ceded all her rights in that vast area to the Union. This move was met by the determined opposition of speculative land companies and other states with their own claims to the same territory. When Virginia's title was duly passed, a committee was appointed to prepare a plan for the temporary government of the Northwest Territory, with Jefferson as chairman. His report, brought in on March 22nd and eventually known as the Ordinance of 1784, was one of his most important state papers. It provided for carving the territory into states, for the establishment of temporary governments, and for the adoption of a written constitution open to revision by future legislatures. When the population of any new state reached twenty thousand, a constitutional convention would be called for the establishment of a permanent government. States were to be divided into counties and each county into townships.

Jefferson, the constructive statesman, found the opportunity of creating new states out of trans-Allegheny land a congenial task. The heart of Jefferson's report lay in his conditions for the establishment of permanent governments. First, "they shall forever remain a part of the United States"; second, "they shall be subject to the Government of the United States in Congress assembled and to the Articles of Confederation"; third, "they shall be subject to pay a part of the national debt"; fourth, "these governments shall be republican in form"; and fifth, "after the year 1800 there shall be neither slavery nor involuntary servitude in any of the said States, otherwise in punishment for crime." The South reacted promptly and violently, and succeeded in striking out the slavery prohibition clause. On April 23rd the Ordinance of 1784, which gave an organized society to future western states, passed with only South Carolina in dissent.

An infinite variety of other projects engaged Jefferson's crowded, six-month career in Congress at Annapolis. By virtue of his wide-ranging mind and versatility of talents he had assumed a position of commanding leadership among all his colleagues. He was placed on every important committee, served as chairman of most of them, and wrote almost all of the important public papers to come out of this Congress. With equal knowledge and experience he ranged between treaties of peace to treatises on commerce, from organizing state governments in the west to arranging the state *occasion of Washington's renunciation of his command, from commercial treaties to currency systems, from individual canal routes to collective executive powers. With a stroke of genius he developed in a report a decimal system of coinage, making the Spanish dollar the base money unit of the nation, together with a gold piece worth ten dollars, a silver dime, and a copper cent: he insisted on the simplification of the arithmetic of coins for the average man, and has ever since been known as the "Father of the Dollar." The remarkable feature and common denominator of all of these reports and bills was Jefferson's motivation to consolidate and strengthen the federal union of states.*

Congress decided on May 7, 1784, to send Jefferson abroad to join Franklin and Adams as ministers plenipotentiary in the negotiation of commercial treaties; he accepted the post with eagerness. He decided to take Patsy with him, leaving the two younger daughters at home in the care of relatives, and selected William Short to accompany him as secretary. He quit Annapolis and Congress on May 11, 1784, and at once made preparations for his departure. Few, if any, Americans were better qualified to represent America abroad than Jefferson, who had so brilliantly served the past two years in Congress. He was forty-one years of age and a new, even if older, world summoned him.

CHAPTER VII

AMERICAN
MINISTER IN FRANCE
(1784–1789)

O<small>N</small> *the morning of July 5, 1784, Jefferson sailed out of Boston Harbor on the fine new merchantman* Ceres, *owned by Nathaniel Tracy of Newburyport. On board with Jefferson was his daughter Patsy—who was now approaching her twelfth birthday—a couple of servants, and six other passengers. Happily, the voyage was calm, pleasant, and surprisingly rapid. They landed at West Cowes on the Isle of Wight on July 26th, were delayed a week in Portsmouth by the slight illness of his daughter, and then went directly to Paris, where the party arrived on August 6.*

It was some time before Jefferson felt entirely at home in Parisian life and society. Even though he read French fluently and discoursed with numerous Frenchmen in the United States, he encountered considerable difficulty in understanding them on their native soil: "I understand the French so imperfectly," he wrote William Temple Franklin in August 1784, "as to be incertain whether those to whom I speak and myself mean the same thing." Accustomed to the serenity of Monticello, the noise and confusion in a city given to frivolity and pleasure disturbed his passion to work intensively and to meditate undisturbed by visitors. Therefore, in addition to his house, which he shared with assistants on the Ameri-

can mission, he rented rooms in a monastery where he found it convenient to work on public documents and official correspondence.

During his first year of residence in France, Jefferson complained most bitterly that the meager sums which a grudging Congress appropriated to the maintenance of its representatives abroad could not begin to pay for living expenses. With the cost of his staff, house rent, transportation, food, drink, clothes, accoutrements, Patsy's education and keep, he felt severely handicapped and humiliated because of the lack of means for maintaining his country's dignity. A true son of Virginia, he was accustomed to entertaining generously: hospitality was considered a duty as much as a pleasure. In some embarrassment he wrote Monroe in June 1785:

I thank you for your attention to my outfit for the articles of household furniture, clothes and a carriage. I have already paid twenty eight thousand livres and have still more to pay. For the greatest part of this I have been obliged to anticipate my salary from which however I shall never be able to repay it. I find that by a rigid economy bordering however on meanness I can save perhaps five hundred livres a month in the summer at least. The residue goes for expences so much of course and of necessity that I cannot avoid them without abandoning all respect to my public character. Yet I will pray you to touch this string which I know to be a tender one with Congress with the utmost delicacy. I had rather be ruined in my fortune than in their esteem. If they allow me half a year's salary as an outfit I can get thro my debts in time. If they raise the salary to what it was or even pay our house rent and taxes I can live with more decency. I trust that Mr. Adams's house at the Hague and Doctor Franklin's at Passy the rent of which has been always paid will give just expectations of the same allowance to me.

There was an element of cruel irony in Jefferson's mission to France, where, while laying the framework of commercial treaties and alliances of the United States, he was reduced to paying for the privilege at a sacrifice that left him in strained circumstances.

Early in 1785 the veteran Franklin, now infirm with age, resigned his post as minister plenipotentiary to the Court of France; in March Congress appointed Jefferson to succeed him. At the same time John Adams was appointed to the Court of St. James'; Jefferson, therefore, was left officially in charge of America's diplomatic relations with France. Since the Paris legation was in reality the headquarters of American diplomacy, he assumed the major responsibilities—and problems—of conducting the foreign relations of the United States during the Confederation Period. Summing up his activities in Paris in his Autobiography, *he said with too much modesty:*

My duties at Paris were confined to a few objects; the receipt of our whale-oils, salted fish, and salted meats on favorable terms, the admission of our rice on equal terms with that of Piedmont, Egypt & the Levant, a mitigation of the monopolies of our tobacco by the Farmers-general, and a free admission of our productions into their islands; were the principal commercial objects which required attention; and on these occasions I was powerfully aided by all the influence and the energies of the Marquis de La Fayette, who proved himself equally zealous for the friendship and welfare of both nations; and in justice I must also say that I found the government entirely disposed to befriend us on all occasions, and to yield us every indulgence not absolutely injurious to themselves.

Franklin was a difficult man to follow; his wit and wisdom, his statesmanship and tact had won him the admiration of all France. "When he left Passy," Jefferson remembered, "it seemed as if the village had lost its patriarch."

The succession to Dr. Franklin at the court of France was an excellent school of humility. On being presented to anyone as the minister of America, the common place question used in such cases was 'C'est vous, Monsieur, qui remplace le Docteur Franklin?'—'It is you, sir, who replace Dr. Franklin?' I generally answered, 'No one can replace him, sir; I am only his successor.'

He was a worthy successor; even though less gay, less easy-going, less cynical, he was certainly from the same school of political ideology as Franklin, and shared his interest in science and technology. In his obstinate and patient endeavor to obtain for the United States commercial rights, and even privileges, that would enable her to pay off her debts to European bankers, Jefferson was earnest but prudent, candid but careful not to offend, with

Gate at Versailles.

a balanced sense of his diplomatic position which prevented zeal from overtaking discretion.

Charles Gravier, Comte de Vergennes, around whose figure American diplomacy on the Continent gravitated, was an extremely interesting man. To avenge former defeats at the hands of England, he had brought France into the war on the side of America almost singlehanded; in spite of some rebuffs he had received through secret negotiations between America and England on the terms of a peace treaty, he still conceived himself to be a friend of America. After a considerable acquaintance, Jefferson was able to estimate his character with some correctness in a letter of January 30, 1787, to Madison.

He is a great Minister in European affairs but has very imperfect ideas of ours [and] no confidence in them. His devotion to the principles of pure despotism render him unaffectionate to our governments but his fear of England makes him value us as a make weight. He is cool, reserved in political conversation, free and familiar on other subjects, and a very attentive, aggreeable person to do business with. It is impossible to have a clearer, better organised head but age has chilled his heart.

Jefferson was to have the best possible relations with Vergennes until that statesman's death. He had no illusions about the minister and knew him to be distinctly reactionary, cynical toward democracy, and skeptical about the future of the United States.

The commercial matters of which Jefferson had to treat with Vergennes were of desperate importance to the economic development and future of the young nation. With skill and patience he worked to abolish the monopoly of the farmers-general over tobacco imports into France, to gain concessions and general exemptions for Americans in shipping products to France, and to enable consumers here to buy directly from France manufactured products.

Jefferson finally achieved his purpose, indirectly but very effectively, through steady pressure and through the unrelenting efforts of Lafayette. The new regulations breaking customs barriers and obtaining free entrance for the products of American farms, fisheries, and infant industries did much, in his view, to free this country from her commercial subservience to Great Britain.

The history of these negotiations involving the debt and commerce of the United States over the next several years is a long and complicated story; if not one of the more dramatic episodes of Jefferson's long career, this period of financial diplomacy at least reveals something of his sense of duty, his industry, his political vision, and his sense of monetary responsibility. Through sheer persistency and hard work, at a personal risk and at a critical moment, he had saved the credit and honor of his country. In spite of tremendous handicaps, due in large part to the apathy of Congress, he had played a brilliant part in laying the foundation of this new nation's international policy and set for the future the highest standard of dignified diplomacy.

If in his official duties as an American minister at a foreign court Jefferson held to a consistent position, advanced for its day in its international point of view and its support of

loosened trade restrictions between nations, he was in his private life as observer and traveler in France wildly ambivalent. A famous letter to Charles Bellini, an Italian who had emigrated to Virginia and became a member of Jefferson's household before being appointed a professor of modern languages at the College of William and Mary, sums up Jefferson's impressions of France about a year after his arrival.

Behold me at length on the vaunted scene of Europe! It is not necessary for your information that I should enter into details concerning it. But you are perhaps curious to know how this new scene has struck a savage of the mountains of America. Not advantageously I assure you. I find the general fate of humanity here most deplorable. The truth of Voltaire's observation offers itself perpetually, that every man here must be either the hammer or the anvil. It is a true picture of that country to which they say we shall pass hereafter, and where we are to see god and his angels in splendor, and crouds of the damned trampled under their feet. While the great mass of the people are thus suffering under physical and moral oppression, I have endeavored to examine more nearly the condition of the great, to appreciate the true value of the circumstances in their situation which dazzle the bulk of the spectators, and especially to compare it with that degree of happiness which is enjoyed in America by every class of people. Intrigues of love occupy the younger, and those of ambition the more elderly part of the great. Conjugal love having no existence among them, domestic happiness, of which that is the basis, is utterly unknown. In lieu of this are substituted pursuits which nourish and invigorate all our bad passions, and which offer only moments of extasy amidst days and months of

Meeting room in Independence Hall, where the delegates of twelve colonies
(New York abstaining) resolved on July 2, 1776, "That these United Colonies are,
and of Right ought to be Free and Independent States."

The gardens of Versailles. Jefferson was frequently at Versailles, as both
an accredited diplomat dealing with the French government,
and an interested observer during the first stages of the French Revolution.

restlessness and torment. Much, very much inferior this to the tranquil permanent felicity with which domestic society in America blesses most of it's inhabitants, leaving them to follow steadily those pursuits which health and reason approve, and rendering truly delicious the intervals of these pursuits.

On some points, however, he was prepared to admit that Europeans have a decided superiority over Americans: their "polite manners," for example, made a deep impression on him:

With respect to what are termed polite manners, without sacrificing too much the sincerity of language, I would wish [my] countrymen to adopt just so much of European politeness as to be ready [to] make all those little sacrifices of self which really render European manners amiable, and relieve society from the disagreeable scenes to which rudeness often exposes it. Here it seems that a man might pass a life without encountering a single rudeness. In the pleasures of the table they are far before us, because with good taste they unite temperance. They do not terminate the most sociable meals by transforming themselves into brutes. I have never yet seen a man drunk in France, even among the lowest of the people.

In science and literature, the situation was different and slightly more complicated:

In science, the mass of people is two centuries behind ours, their literati half a dozen years before us. Books, really good, acquire just reputation in that time, and so become known to us and communicate to us all their advances in knowlege. Is not this delay compensated by our being placed out of the reach of that swarm of nonsense which issues daily from a thousand presses and perishes almost in issuing?

Finally, in the arts there was no possible comparison:

Were I to proceed to tell you how much I enjoy their architecture, sculpture, painting, music, I should want words. It is in these arts they shine. The last of them particularly is an enjoiment, the deprivation of which with us cannot be calculated. I am almost ready to say it is the only thing which from my heart I envy them, and which in spight of all the authority of the decalogue I do covet.

On another subject he was more direct in his comparison between the two countries. France's main problem was one of involuntary poverty; the people had been expropriated from the land and huddled into vast exploitable masses. "The property of this country is absolutely concentrated in a very few hands, having revenues of from half a million guineas a year downwards": the result was that the majority of the people lived merely on sufferance. This state of affairs was new to Jefferson and appalled him. Fresh from the spaciousness of America, where institutions were liberal and progressive and poverty practically unknown, the contrasts between the swarming alleys of Paris and the resplendent life at the Court, between the hopeless masses and the feudal regime, filled him with a sense of horror.

The more he saw of the conditions in Europe, the more he became homesick and nostalgic for his native Virginia. Conditions there only strengthened his love for his own country. To Baron Geismer, the former Hessian prisoner of war in Charlottesville, he wrote in September 1785:

I am now of an age which does not easily accomodate itself to new manners and new modes of living: and I am savage enough to prefer the woods, the wilds, and the independance of Monticello, to all the brilliant pleasures of this gay capital. I shall therefore rejoin myself to my native country with new attachments, with exaggerated esteem for it's advantages, for tho' there is less wealth there, there is more freedom, more ease and less misery.

However, Jefferson genuinely liked the French people, in contrast to the English, and increasingly came to feel drawn to them and attracted to their way of life; when he did return to America, he looked upon France as his second home. To Abigail Adams, then with her husband in London, he wrote in a lighthearted spirit in June 1785:

I consider your boasts of the splendour of your city and of it's superb hackney coaches as

The Tuileries.

The Louvre.

a flout, and declaring that I would not give the polite, self-denying, feeling, hospitable, good-humoured people of this country and their amability in every point of view, (tho' it must be confessed our streets are somewhat dirty, and our fiacres rather indifferent) for ten such races of rich, proud, hectoring, swearing, squibbing, carnivorous animals as those among whom you are; and that I do love this *people* with all my heart, and think that with a better religion and a better form of govern-

ment and their present governors their condition and country would be most enviable. I pray you to observe that I have used the term *people* and that this is a noun of the masculine as well as feminine gender.

There was in Jefferson's mind a polarity between the Old World and the New, between Europe and America, and he viewed with stern disfavor the influence of European life and manners on the minds and morality of young

Americans. He regarded, moreover, the emergence of the liberated wife and the political woman with profound distrust. After four years' experience in France he wrote to President Washington that without the evidence of one's own eyes one could hardly "believe in the desperate state to which things are reduced in this country from the omnipotence of an influence which, fortunately for the happiness of the sex itself, does not endeavour to extend itself in our country beyond the domestic line." He was continually shocked by the coarseness and vulgarity, let alone the scandal, of French women around the circle of public officials, and he was outraged to observe that "their solicitations bid defiance to laws and regulations." For the dazzling and celebrated beauty, Mrs. William Bingham, he provided after her return to America the daily itinerary of a fashionable Parisienne, in all its idleness and futility, in a lively letter dated February 7, 1787:

You are then engaged to tell me truly and honestly whether you do not find the tranquil pleasures of America preferable to the empty bustle of Paris. For to what does that bustle tend? At eleven o'clock it is day chez Madame. The curtains are drawn. Propped on bolsters and pillows, and her head scratched into a little order, the bulletins of the sick are read, and the billets of the well. She writes to some of her acquaintance and receives the visits of others. If the morning is not very thronged, she is able to get out and hobble round the cage of the Palais royal: but she must hobble quickly, for the Coeffeur's turn is come; and a tremendous turn it is! Happy, if he does not make her arrive when dinner is half over! The torpitude of digestion a little passed, she flutters half an hour thro' the streets by way of paying visits, and then to the Spectacles. These finished, another half hour is devoted to dodging in and out of the doors of her very sincere friends, and away to supper. After supper cards; and after cards bed, to rise at noon the next day, and to tread, like a mill-horse, the same trodden circle over again. . . .

In America, on the other hand, the society of your husband, the fond cares for the children, the arrangements of the house, the improvements of the grounds fill every moment with a healthy and an useful activity. Every exertion is encouraging, because to present amusement it joins the promise of some future good. The intervals of leisure are filled by the society of real friends, whose affections are not thinned to cob-web by being spread over a thousand objects.

Mrs. Bingham was a worthy adversary and answered in June: "I agree with you that many of the fashionable pursuits of the Parisian Ladies are rather frivolous, and become uninteresting to a reflective Mind; but the Picture you have exhibited, is rather overcharged. You have thrown a strong light upon all that is ridiculous in their Characters, and you have buried their good Qualities in the Shade. . . .

"The Arts of Elegance are there considered essential, and are carried to a state of Perfection; the Mind is continually gratified with the admiration of Works of Taste. I have the pleasure of knowing you too well, to doubt of your subscribing to this opinion."

"Our good ladies, I trust have been too wise to wrinkle their foreheads with politics," he replied somewhat anxiously to the skittish Mrs. Bingham. "They are contented to soothe and calm the minds of their husbands returning ruffled from political debate."

Negotiations with France, England, and the Barbary States proceeded at a leisurely pace, and there were long intervals during which Jefferson found time to carry on an extensive

Jefferson, while at Paris, was "violently smitten with the hotel de Salm."

Bagatelle, built by Comte d'Artois.

correspondence and to investigate the state of the arts and sciences of France and England. He had hardly settled in Paris when he was reporting to leading figures in early American science on a variety of new inventions and technological advances in France. He informed Madison in November 1784 "of some Phosphoretic matches." He was impressed by their usefulness.

By having them at your bedside with a candle, the latter may be lighted at any moment of the night without getting out of bed. By keeping them on your writing table, you may seal three or four letters with one of them, or light a candle if you want to seal more which in the summer is convenient. In the woods they supply the want of steel, flint and punk.

He had also recently seen a newly invented Argand lamp:

There is a new lamp invented here lately which with a very small consumption of oil

Parc de Bagatelle, visited by Jefferson with Maria Cosway.

(of olives) is thought to give a light equal to six or eight candles. The wick is hollow in the middle in the form of a hollow cylinder, and permits the air to pass up thro' it. It requires no snuffing. They make shade candlesticks of them at two guineas price, which are excellent for reading and are much used by studious men.

He was delighted with a copying press he had recently acquired, and wrote Madison in September 1785, offering to send him one like it:

Have you a copying press? If you have not, you should get one. Mine (exclusive of paper which costs a guinea a ream) has cost me about 14. guineas. I would give ten times that sum that I had had it from the date of the stamp act.

He was fascinated with the possibilities of the newly invented balloon for human ascensions. He reported to Charles Thomson with avid delight of some successful experiments outside of Paris:

Two artists at Javel, about 4 miles hence, are pursuing the art of directing the baloon. They ascend and descend at will, without expending their gaz, and they can deflect 45°. from the course of the wind when it is not very strong. We may certainly expect that this desideratum will be found. As the birds and fish prove that the means exist, we may count on human ingenuity for it's discovery.

A tour of an arms factory where muskets were assembled from interchangeable parts demonstrated to Jefferson the possibilities of human ingenuity and the promise of assembly line techniques in manufacturing.

An improvement is made here in the construction of the musket which it may be interesting to Congress to know, should they at any time propose to procure any. It consists in the making every part of them so exactly alike that what belongs to any one, may be used for every other musket in the magazine. The government here has examined and approved the method, and is establishing a large manufactory for the purpose. As yet the inventor has only completed the lock of the musket on this plan. He will proceed immediately to have the barrel, stock, and their parts executed in the same way. Supposing it might be useful to the U.S., I went to the workman, he presented me the parts of 50. locks taken to peices, and arranged in compartments. I put several together myself taking peices at hazard as they came to hand, and they fitted in the most perfect manner. The advantages of this, when arms need repair, are evident. He effects it by tools of his own contrivance which at the same time abridge the work so that he thinks he shall be able to furnish the musket two livres cheaper than the common price. But it will be two or three years before he will be able to furnish any quantity. I mention it now, as it may have influence on the plan for furnishing our magazines with this arm.

All things mechanical aroused Jefferson's attention, and the progress of science enraptured him. He was profoundly convinced that theoretical and applied science would eventually enlarge men's minds and ease their toil. To the Reverend James Madison, the president of the College of William and Mary, he wrote on July 19, 1788:

As you seem willing to accept of the crums of science on which we are subsisting here, it is with pleasure I continue to hand them on to you in proportion as they are dealt out. Herschel's volcano in the moon you have doubtless heard of, and placed among the other vagaries of a head which seems not organised for sound induction. . . . You know also that Doctor Ingenhousz had discovered, as he supposed, from experiment, that vegetation might be promoted by occasioning streams of the electrical fluid to pass through a plant, and that other Physicians had received and confirmed his theory. . . . Speaking one day with Monsieur de Buffon on the present ardor of chemical enquiry, he affected to consider chemistry but as cookery, and to place the toils of the laboratory on a footing with those of the kitchen. I think it on the contrary among the most useful of sciences, and big with future discoveries for the utility and safety of the human race.

To Joseph Willard at Harvard College he continued on this same theme in March 1789:

What a feild have we at our doors to signalize ourselves in! The botany of America is far from being exhausted: it's Mineralogy is untouched, and it's Natural history or Zoology totally mistaken and misrepresented. As far as I have seen there is not one single species of terrestrial birds common to Europe and America, and I question if there be a single species of quadrupeds. (Domestic animals are to be excepted.) It is for such institutions as that over which you preside so worthily, Sir, to do justice to our country, it's productions, and it's genius. It is the work to which the young men, whom you are forming, should lay their hands. We have spent the prime of our lives in procuring them the precious blessing of liberty. Let them spend theirs in shewing that it is the great parent of science and of virtue; and that a nation will be great in both always in proportion as it is free.

During the summer of 1785, *a request came to Jefferson from the Virginia Assembly to consult with an able architect in order to draft plans for a new capitol building in Richmond. Few assignments could possibly have pleased him any more than this one. He searched out Charles Louis Clérisseau, author of* Monuments de Nîmes *and an architect steeped in antiquity, who collaborated with Jefferson on the model and plans in the early stages; the final product, however, was Jefferson's own. The Maison Carrée at Nîmes, which Jefferson had not yet seen except in drawings, represented to him the ultimate in architectural splendor, and became the basis for his drawings.*

I was written to in 1785 (being then in Paris) by Directors appointed to superintend the building of a Capitol in Richmond, to advise them as to a plan, and to add to it one of a prison. Thinking it a favorable opportunity of introducing into the state an example of architecture in the classic style of antiquity, and the Maison quarrée of Nismes, an antient Roman temple, being considered as the most perfect model existing of what may be called Cubic architecture, I applied to M. Clerissault, who had published drawings of the Antiquities of Nismes, to have me a model of the building made in stucco, only changing the order from Corinthian to Ionic, on account of the difficulty of the Corinthian capitals. I yielded with reluctance to the taste of Clerissault, in his preference of the modern capital of Scamozzi to the more noble capital of antiquity. This was executed by the artist whom Choiseul Gouffier had carried with him to Constantinople, and employed while Ambassador there, in making those beautiful models of the remains of Grecian architecture which are to be seen at Paris. To adapt the exterior to our use, I drew

The Maison Carrée at Nîmes.

The state capitol at Richmond.

a plan for the interior, with the apartments necessary for legislative, executive & judiciary purposes, and accommodated in their size and distribution to the form and dimensions of the building. These were forwarded to the Directors in 1786. and were carried into execution, with some variations not for the better, the most important of which however admit of future correction.

He sent his plans in January, and with some reason bragged a little in his letter to James Currie:

I send by this conveiance designs for the

Capitol. They are simple and sublime. More cannot be said. They are not the brat of a whimsical conception never before brought to light, but copied from the most precious the most perfect model of antient architecture remaining on earth; one which has received the approbation of near 2000 years, and which is sufficiently remarkable to have been visited by all travellers.

The capitol, completed after many delays, represents one of Jefferson's greatest achievements as an architect—one of the earliest and finest examples of public buildings in the neoclassical style.

90

CHAPTER VIII

GRAND TOUR
OF ENGLISH GARDENS
(1786)

In March 1786 Jefferson went to London on the urgent request of John Adams, the American minister at the Court of St. James', on a mission which proved to be fruitless and frustrating diplomatically, though pleasant enough horticulturally. The alleged reason given by Adams requesting Jefferson "to come here without loss of Time" concerned the treaty with Portugal which, after long delays, now seemed on the verge of completion. However, the negotiations with the Portuguese minister, Chevalier de Pinto, were of comparatively minor interest to the American commissioners; the all-important business was with the mysterious Tripolitan envoy in London, Abdrahaman, as Jefferson told John Jay on March 12, 1786: "Mr. Adams informing me that there was at this place a minister from Tripoli, having general powers to enter into treaties on behalf of his state . . . and that he gave reason to believe he could also take arrangements with us for Tunis."

This swarthy spokesman of the pirates and unabashed blackmailer sat down with Adams and Jefferson and smugly unfolded the horrendous and unsavory details of the corsairs' invincibility and admitted cruelty to prisoners of war along the Mediterranean Coast. They learned of American sailors held captive who were forced to perform slave labor, "carrying Rocks and Timber on their backs for nine miles out of the Country." The wily Tripolitan ambassador then smiled ingratiatingly and named his price for protection from seizure of American merchant vessels by the Barbary states.

Vergennes warned Jefferson "that money and fear are the two only agents at Algiers." But what to do? The Americans could neither meet the financial demands of the pirates nor threaten to counter shipping interference with a retaliatory naval strike. Jefferson posed the dilemma to Elbridge Gerry: "But what will you do with the pyratical states? Buy a peace at their enormous price; force one; or abandon the carriage into the Mediterranean to other powers? All these measures are disagreeable." Faced with humiliation and filled with outrage by this assertive lawlessness, Jefferson was more belligerent than Adams and recommended a war of retaliation against the Algerians, and in so doing advocated the beginning of the American navy. In July 1786 Jefferson wrote Adams:

I acknolege I very early thought it would be best to effect a peace thro' the medium of war. . . . However if it is decided that we shall buy a peace, I know no reason for delaying the operation, but should rather think it ought to be hastened. But I should prefer the obtaining it by war.... If it be admitted however that war, on the fairest prospects, is still exposed to incertainties, I weigh against this the greater incertainty of the duration of a peace bought with money, from such a people, from a **Dey** 80. years old, and by a nation who, on the hypothesis of buying peace, is to have no power on the sea to enforce an observance of it.

It was to take many years of negotiations and a war before the Barbary powers were finally taught to refrain from molesting American ships. On January 3, 1797, a treaty between the United States and Tripoli was finally concluded and signed.

The Portuguese affair, however, was concluded and settled for the moment much more smoothly; the two American commissioners then turned their attention on England herself. When they met with officials of the government and "some of the most distinguished mercantile characters," Jefferson had no illusions about any possible degree of success in the negotiations, and the meeting only served to strengthen his hatred of England.

Our conferences were intended as preparatory to some arrangement. It is uncertain how far we should have been able to accommodate our opinions. But the absolute aversion of the government to enter into any arrangement, prevented the object from being pursued. Each country is left to do justice to itself and to the other, from being according to its own ideas as to what is past, and to scramble for the future as well as they can, to regulate their commerce by duties and prohibitions, and perhaps by cannons and mortars—in which event we must abandon the ocean, where we are weak.

The arrogance of the British and the boorish behavior of the king when Adams duly presented Jefferson at court to the king and queen was an infuriating experience; it rankled in Jefferson's heart until the very end of his life. In his old age he wrote in his Autobiography:

On my presentation as usual to the King and Queen at their levées, it was impossible for anything to be more ungracious than their notice of Mr. Adams & myself. I saw at once that the ulcerations in the narrow mind of that mulish being left nothing to be expected on the subject of my attendance.

Charles Francis Adams, John Adams' grandson and American ambassador to the Court of St. James' during the Civil War, discovered evidence years later why this snub inflicted on Adams and Jefferson was so painful and bitter: "The King turned his back upon our American commissioners, a hint, which of course, was not lost upon the circle of subjects in attendance." And when, a few days later, Jefferson was received by the Marquis of Carmarthen, the minister of foreign affairs, he noted with some sense of wounded pride that

the distance and disinclination which he betrayed in his conversation, the vagueness & evasions of his answers to us, confirmed me in the belief of their aversion to have anything to do with us. We delivered him however our Projét, Mr. Adams not despairing as much as I did of it's effect.

For seven weeks that remained to Jefferson in England, he and Adams were never able to gain an audience with the foreign minister again, though "we afterwards, by one or more notes, requested his appointment of an interview and conference, which, without directly declining, he evaded by pretences of other pressing occupations for the moment." It is not surprising that Jefferson was so incensed by the English that he was driven to exclaim in a letter to William Stephens Smith that "of all nations on earth, they require to be treated with the utmost hauteur. They require to be kicked into good common manners." Despite his aversion to the British and his distaste for ceremonies, he was willing to do his best, if only to "put an end to all further expectations on our side the water, and shew that the time is come for doing whatever is to be done by us for counteracting the unjust and greedy designs of this country."

In the middle of these negotiations with various envoys and ministers—with all of the weariness of body, exacerbation of mind, and bitterness of spirit—Jefferson and Adams decided they needed a vacation. Jefferson expected to remain in England but a short time, and as all of the negotiations dragged out, he determined to fulfill one private ambition: to see some of the famous English gardens. Fifteen years earlier he had studied intently the various gardening books available in Virginia, notably Thomas Whately's Observations on Modern Gardening, *and had attempted to follow their precepts in laying out his own gardens at Monticello. In company with Adams, he set off on April 2, 1786, by post chaise for a grand tour of the most celebrated gardens that lay along the Thames and its tributaries west of London. Jefferson summed up his impressions in a letter to John Page in early May shortly after his return to Paris: "The gardening in that country is the article in which it surpasses all the earth. I mean their pleasure gardening. This indeed went far beyond my ideas."*

The reactions and comments of these two rustic republicans from America, viewing together the noble piles and luxuriant gardens where the aristocracy of England took their ease and pleasure, reveal as few other episodes in their long careers the different ways in which they viewed the same shared experiences. Adams was plainly attracted to the aristocratic seats and enjoyed the visual, sensual qualities of their luxurious architecture, paintings, statuary, plants, and poetry; yet his secular puritanical strain prevented him from allowing himself to be carried away by this emotional attraction to art. After all, "Ridings, Parks, Pleasure Grounds, Gardens and ornamented Farms" could create a tremendous national debt in America. Jefferson had no such qualms; with a copy of Whately in hand, he observed everything with energy and determination, comparing the originals with their descriptions and investigating the chances of planting similar plants and gardens in America.

I always walked over the gardens with his book in my hand, examined with attention the particular spots he described, found them so justly characterised by him as to be easily recognised, and saw with wonder, that his fine imagination had never been able to seduce him from the truth. My enquiries were directed chiefly to such practical things as might enable me to estimate the expence of making and maintaining a garden in that style.

The first day they visited no less than six country seats, beginning with Chiswick, the magnificent Palladian villa built by Lord Burlington, where Jefferson was repelled by the sumptuous decoration and reckless luxury, and commented:

The Octagonal dome has an ill effect, both within and without; the garden shews still too

Chiswick, the Palladian sculpture garden built by Lord Burlington.

The south front of Stowe, owned by the Marquis of Buckingham.

much of art; an obelisk of very ill effect. Another in the middle of a pond useless.

At Hampton Court, the largest and handsomest of the royal palaces, he observed: "Old fashioned. Clipt yews grown wild." At Wotton, a property of the Marquis of Buckingham, the extended use of water in the gardens was the outstanding feature:

The lake covers 50. a[cre]s. the river 5. as. the bason 15. as. the little river 2. as. = 72. as. of water. The lake and great river are on a level. They fall into the bason 5. f. below, and that again into the little river 5. f. lower. These waters lie in form of an L. The house is in middle of open side, forming the angle. A walk goes round the whole, 3. miles in circumference, and containing within it about 300. as. Sometimes it passes close to the water, sometimes so far off as to leave large pasture ground between it and water. But 2. hands to keep the pleasure grounds in order. Much neglected. The water affords 2000. brace of carp a year. There is a Palladian bridge of which I think Whateley does not speak.

On April 2nd Jefferson and Adams visited two places that represent the greatest possible extremes to imagine: the palatial and magnificent Stowe and Shakespeare's humble birthplace. The gardens at Stowe were among the

Temple by a lake in the extensive gardens at Stowe, the most celebrated in Georgian England.

most celebrated in Georgian England and were described at some length by Jefferson:

15. men and 18. boys employed in keeping pleasure grounds. Within the Walk are considerable portions separated by inclosures and used for pasture. The Egyptian pyramid is almost entirely taken down by the late Ld. Temple to erect a building there, in commemoration of Mr. Pitt, but he died before beginning it, and nothing is done to it yet. The grotto, and two rotundas are taken away. There are 4. levels of water, receiving it one from the other. The bason contains 7. as. the lake below that 10. as. Kent's building is called the temple of Venus. The inclosure is entirely by ha! ha! At each end of the front line there is a recess like the bastion of a fort. In one of these is the temple of Friendship, in the other the temple of Venus. They are seen the one from the other, the line of sight passing, not thro' the garden, but through the country parallel to the line of the garden. This has a good effect. In the approach to Stowe, you are brought a mile through a straight avenue, pointing to the Corinthian arch and to the house, till you get to the Arch. Then you turn short to the right. The straight approach is very ill. The Corinthian arch has a very useless appearance, inasmuch as it has no pretension to any destina-

The maze at Hampton Court, the model for the one behind the Governor's Palace in Williamsburg.

Hampton Court, the largest and handsomest of the royal palaces, though Jefferson termed it "old fashioned" when he visited it with John Adams in April 1786.

Blenheim, a "truly princely habitation" as Thomas Whately called it, interested Jefferson chiefly for its gardens, the design of which he later incorporated at Monticello.

tion. Instead of being an object from the house, it is an obstacle to a very pleasing distant prospect. The Graecian valley being clear of trees, while the hill on each side is covered with them, is much deepened to appearance.

At Stratford-on-Avon, where Adams was more vocal in his comments, Jefferson only notes in his accounts paying a shilling "for seeing house where Shakespeare was born" and another for "seeing his tombstone."

At Blenheim Jefferson was more interested in the gardens, and the two hundred people employed to maintain them, than the famous castle, which overpowered and dazzled most ordinary visitors.

The water here is very beautiful, and very grand. The cascade from the lake a fine one. Except this the garden has no great beauties. It is not laid out in fine lawns and woods, but the trees are scattered thinly over the ground,

The gardens at Kew, transformed by Sir William Chambers into the picturesque style.

and every here and there small thickets of shrubs, in oval raised beds, cultivated, and flowers among the shrubs. The gravelled walks are broad. Art appears too much.

Jefferson was back in London on April 10th, having partially satisfied his appetite for sight-seeing. He did take a short excursion out of the city to visit Kew Gardens in Surrey, but what interested him more than the buildings in an assortment of revival styles was a screw for raising water to a higher level, designed on the principle established by Archimedes. Here was something that delighted his mechanical mind, and he took notes and made sketches for its possibilities at home.

On April 26th Jefferson quit London, never to return, with a feeling of complete futility and despondency over the English situation.

All of his previous prejudices had been confirmed, and in addition he had acquired a few new ones. He could still speak of the British with the same cold contempt as "our natural enemies, and as the only nation on earth who wish us ill from the bottom of their souls. And I am satisfied that were our continent to be swallowed up by the ocean, Great Britain would be in a bonfire from one end to the other." When the Comte de Moustier was appointed French minister to the United States, Jefferson took the occasion to write him in October 1787 that he would "find the affections of the Americans with France, but their habits with England. Chained to that country by circumstances, embracing what they loathe, they realize the fable of the living and dead found together."

CHAPTER IX

JOURNEY
TO SOUTHERN FRANCE
AND ITALIAN
RICE COUNTRY (1787)

Some *two months after his return to Paris, Jefferson wrote with whimsical exaggeration to John Adams: "I am meditating what step to take to provoke a letter from Mrs. Adams, from whom my files inform me I have not received one these hundred years." Even though Jefferson returned to Paris disgruntled and disillusioned with so much that he had experienced in England, he brought back an intangible, lasting possession that he would treasure for life: this was a firm, rich friendship with John and Abigail Adams. An acquaintance of several months, begun during the stay of the Adamses in France, ripened into friendship during several weeks in London.*

During his stay in Paris, the shy widower gradually, if only partially, emerged from his cloistered routine of a strictly disciplined life and allowed himself selective associations with female society. For three or four years following his wife's death, Jefferson had, in his grief and sorrow, repressed his emotions and tended largely to base his female friendships on common intellectual interests and pursuits with the wives of close friends. Not surprisingly, these were safe, comfortable, highly respect-

able, thoroughly American friendships, which were without any of the overtones of liaisons so common in late-eighteenth-century French society.

But some time after he returned from England to Paris he fell in love with the young, beautiful, and vivacious Maria Cosway, the wife of a well-known English painter, who was herself distinguished not only as a gifted miniature painter but also as a talented musician. By all accounts she was a great beauty and the forty-three-year-old widower was smitten hard by the delicately chiseled facial features and gentle disposition of the twenty-seven-year-old artist. He met the Cosways during their short stay in Paris through John Trumbull, the American artist, and his circle of artist-friends; there is every indication that Jefferson found the charm of the young woman irresistible. The fires of romance blazed up strongly and dangerously for the few short weeks that remained to them, during which time he contrived to be with her almost daily. When she did return to England in October 1786, he was overcome with emotion and wrote her a long love letter in the form of an essay on friend-

ship, now famous, which he called a "dialogue between my Head and my Heart."

Having performed the last sad office of handing you into your carriage at the Pavillon de St. Denis, and seen the wheels get actually into motion, I turned on my heel and walked, more dead than alive, to the opposite door, where my own was awaiting me. . . . Seated by my fire side, solitary and sad, the following dialogue took place between my Head and my Heart.

Head. Well, friend, you seem to be in a pretty trim.

Heart. I am indeed the most wretched of all earthly beings. Overwhelmed with grief, every fibre of my frame distended beyond it's natural powers to bear, I would willingly meet whatever catastrophe should leave me no more to feel or to fear.

Head. These are the eternal consequences of your warmth and precipitation. This is one of the scrapes into which you are ever leading us. You confess your follies indeed: but still you hug and cherish them, and no reformation can be hoped, where there is no repentance. . . . I often told you . . . that you were imprudently engaging your affections under circumstances that must cost you a great deal of pain: that the persons indeed were of the greatest merit, possessing good sense, good humour, honest hearts, honest manners, and eminence in a lovely art: that the lady had moreover qualities and accomplishments, belonging to her sex, which might form a chapter apart for her: such as music, modesty, beauty, and that softness of disposition which is the ornament of her sex and charm of ours. But that all these considerations would increase the pang of separation: that their stay here was to be short: that you rack our whole system when you are parted from those you love, complain-

ing that such a separation is worse than death, inasmuch as this ends our sufferings, whereas that only begins them: and that the separation would in this instance be the more severe as you would probably never see them again.

Heart. But they told me they would come back again the next year.

Head. But in the mean time see what you suffer: and their return too depends on so many circumstances that if you had a grain of prudence you would not count upon it. Upon the whole it is improbable and therefore you should abandon the idea of ever seeing them again.

Heart. May heaven abandon me if I do!

Maria Cosway, who had encouraged the flirtation in Paris, did not continue it from England and her reply to this passionate eighteen-page letter consisted of only four simple, arid lines. It was all over. With the separation of time and distance and neglect, the head became victor over the heart: the vital spark was gone and only a formal friendship—and a memory—survived.

Jefferson's friendship with Abigail Adams, on the other hand, became a source of reflective contentment for him. She also obviously enjoyed her correspondence with him, in which she exchanged a steady stream of news and banter. "I suppose you must have heard the report respecting Col. Smith—that he has taken my daughter from me" in marriage, Mrs. Adams informed him on July 23, 1786; she proposed that Jefferson exchange one of his daughters for one of her sons. "I am for Strengthening [the] federal union," she teased him.

The personal pleasure of this correspondence was suddenly and alarmingly marred in January 1787 with the receipt of news of insurgency in the Adamses' native state. Re-

ports of Shays's Rebellion in the Commonwealth of Massachusetts crackled like summer lightning through the capitals of Europe; Abigail Adams reacted more violently to the armed riots and disturbances than did her husband and wrote apprehensively to Jefferson: "With regard to the Tumults in my Native state which you inquire about, I wish I could say that report had exagerated them. It is too true Sir that they have been carried to so allarming a Height as to stop the Courts of justice in several Counties. Ignorant, wrestless desperadoes, without conscience or principals, have led a deluded multitude to follow their standard, under pretence of grievences which have no existance but in their immaginations. Some of them were crying out for a paper currency, some for an equal distribution of property, some were for annihilating all debts, others complaning that the Senate was a useless Branch of Government, that the Court of common pleas was unnecessary, and that the sitting of the General Court in Boston was a grievence. By this list you will see the materials which compose this rebellion, and the necessity there is of the wisest and most vigorus measures to quell and suppress it. Instead of that laudible spirit which you approve, which makes a people watchfull over their Liberties and alert in the defence of them, these mobish insurgents are for sapping the foundation, and distroying the whole fabrick at once."

Even the normally restrained Reverend James Madison wrote that it looked like "The Beginnings of a civil war there," which "appear to some as Proofs of Instability and misery inseperable from a Republican Government. But to others, who I trust judge better, they appear only as the Symptoms of a strong and healthy Constitution, which, after discharging a few peccant Humours, will be restored to a new Vigour." Jefferson was not alarmed; he was unswervingly of the latter persuasion. In a bold and now famous statement to the other James Madison, he wrote:

I hold it that a little rebellion now and then is a good thing, and as necessary in the political world as storms in the physical. Unsuccesful rebellions indeed generally establish the incroachments on the rights of the people which have produced them. An observation of this truth should render honest republican governors so mild in their punishment of rebellions, as not to discourage them too much. It is a medecine necessary for the sound health of government.

In letters to friends in America during these troubled times, he was developing and articulating his theory of revolution and the liberties of the people. To President Ezra Stiles of Yale College he wrote:

The commotions which have taken place in America, as far as they are yet known to me, offer nothing threatening. They are a proof that the people have liberty enough, and I would not wish them less than they have. If the happiness of the mass of the people can be secured at the expence of a little tempest now and then, or even of a little blood, it will be a precious purchase.

In his own mind he was working out his concept of the relationship between the governors and the governed; he did not believe the state was above or should have an abstract life of its own apart from the people who composed it.

The people are the only censors of their governors: and even their errors will tend to keep these to the true principles of their institution.

Chambertin vineyards, Côte d'Or: "The wines which have given such celebrity to Burgundy grow only on the Cote. . . . They begin at Chambertin."

To punish these errors too severely would be to suppress the only safeguard of the public liberty. The way to prevent these irregular interpositions of the people is to give them full information of their affairs thro' the channel of the public papers, and to contrive that those papers should penetrate the whole mass of the people. The basis of our governments being the opinion of the people, the very first object should be to keep that right; and were it left to me to decide whether we should have a government without newspapers, or newspapers without a government, I should not hesitate a moment to prefer the latter.

These letters, filled with stunning political apothegms, were written while Jefferson was suffering from intense pain in a slow-healing right wrist, which he dislocated in an accident on September 18, 1786. The seeming inability of the swollen wrist to heal obstructed Jefferson's official duties and hindered his personal epistolary duties. He was forced to learn to write with his left hand and to depend upon William Short to transcribe his official correspondence. Nearly five months after the accident Jefferson wrote Madison and explained the plans he finally made:

In a former letter I mentioned to you the dislocation of my wrist. I can make not the least use of it, except for the single article of writing, tho' it is going on five months since the accident happened. I have great anxieties lest I should never recover any considerable use of it. I shall, by the advice of my Surgeons, set out in a fortnight for the waters of Aix in Provence. I chose these out of several they proposed to me, because if they fail to be effectual, my journey will not be useless altogether. It will give me an opportunity of examining the canal of Languedoc and of acquiring knowlege of that species of navigation which may be useful hereafter: but more immediately it will enable me to take the tour of the ports concerned in commerce with us, to examine on the spot the defects of the late regulations respecting our commerce, to learn the further improvements which may be made on it, and, on my return, to get this business finished. I shall be absent between two and three months.

Health and relief he did not find, but the experience for Jefferson proved to be as memorable as it was valuable, particularly since he traveled with notebook in hand. Crops, the condition of the soil, methods of agriculture, the plight and condition of the people, statistics of commerce, manufactures, machinery, forges, bridges, chimneys, sidewalks, pumps, aqueducts, canals—everything that was ingenious and practical—drew his close attention and were entered in his notes in the fullest detail. On the last day of February, Jefferson left Paris in his own carriage, using changes of post horses, and drove up the Seine through Champagne and Burgundy, and then made his way down the Rhône through the Beaujolais by Lyons, Avignon, Nimes, to Aix, where he lingered long enough to try the effect of the waters on his wrist. The bones had not been set properly and the wrist never healed.

Winepress in Clos-de-Vougeot, between Dijon and Beaune.

Orange: "the sublime triumphal arch at the entrance into the city."

At La Fontaine de Vaucluse near Avignon.

Pont St. Esprit over the Rhone River.

At Nîmes Jefferson came to one of the high spots of his journey: here the famous Maison Carrée reared its battered splendor. No serious student of history and architecture could remain indifferent to the majestic ruins of ancient Rome. And Jefferson, like the historian Edward Gibbon a few years before this, succumbed and lost his heart to the moldering beauty of the ruins that were once Rome. He wrote from Nîmes to his Parisian friend Madame de Tessé:

Here I am Madam, gazing whole hours at the Maison quarrée, like a lover at his mistress. The stocking-weavers and silk spinners around it consider me as an hypochondriac Englishman, about to write with a pistol the last chapter of his history. This is the second time I have been in love since I left Paris. The first was with a Diana at the Chateau de Laye Epinaye in the Beaujolois, a delicious morsel of sculpture, by Michael Angelo Slodtz. This, you will say, was in rule, to fall in love with a fine woman: but, with a house! It is out of all precedent! No, madam, it is not without a precedent in my own history. While at Paris, I was violently smitten with the hotel de Salm, and used to go to the Thuileries almost daily to look at it. The loueuse des chaises, inattentive to my passion, never had the complaisance

Pont du Gard: "a sublime antiquity, and well preserved."

to place a chair there; so that, sitting on the parapet, and twisting my neck round to see the object of my admiration, I generally left it with a torticollis. From Lyons to Nismes I have been nourished with the remains of Roman grandeur.

For years Jefferson had pored over drawings and dimensions of the Maison Carrée, particularly within recent months as he drew plans for the Virginia state capitol, and now, at last, he was beholding his "beloved" for the first time. The actuality, he admitted, far surpassed his dreams. His soul melted and his pen was moved to write in dithyrambs. To James Madison he wrote:

It was built by Caius and Lucius Caesar and repaired by Louis XIV. and has the suffrage of all the judges of architecture who have seen it, as yeilding to no one of the beautiful monuments of Greece, Rome, Palmyra and Balbec which late travellers have communicated to us. It is very simple, but it is noble beyond expression, and would have done honour to our country as presenting to travellers a morsel of taste in our infancy promising much for our maturer age.

He assured Edmund Randolph that "in the opinion of all who have seen it yeilds in beauty to no peice of architecture on earth."

It has long been recognized that Jefferson, in his design of the state capitol at Richmond based on the Roman temple of antiquity at Nîmes, introduced the revival of classical architecture in America. More precisely, out of his admiration for the ruins and symbols of

"The precious remains of antiquity" at St. Rémy.

classical antiquity and his preoccupation with
public buildings, he established and refined
the monumental style of antiquity into a new
style, more properly called "romantic classicism." He remained a devout student of the
order, logic, stability, and rationalistic urbanity of classicism; yet with a sensitive un-Au-
gustan exuberance he could exclaim, "Here I
am Madam, gazing whole hours at the Maison quarrée, like a lover at his mistress." Here
speaks the man of sensibility at that critical
hour of transition from the eighteenth to the
nineteenth century, at the dawn of the Age of
Romanticism.

Although Jefferson went to Nîmes ostensi-
bly to visit the Roman antiquities, he was in
truth also engaged in a secret diplomatic mission, which he did not confide to anyone for
six weeks. Finally, early in May he wrote John
Jay in the Continental Congress and revealed
the reason for going to Nîmes.

My journey into this part of the country has
procured me information which I will take the
liberty of communicating to Congress. In
October last I received a letter dated Mont-
pelier Octob. 2. 1786. announcing to me that
the writer was a foreigner who has a matter
of very great consequence to communicate to
me, and desired I would indicate the channel
thro which it might pass safely. I did so. . . .
As by this time I had been advised to try the
waters of Aix, I [wrote] to the gentleman my
design, and that I would go off my road as far
as Nismes, under the pretext of seeing the antiquities of that place, if he would meet me
there. He met me, and the following is the sum
of the information I received from him. 'Brazil

contains as many inhabitants as Portugal. They are 1. Portuguese. 2. Native whites. 3. black and mulatto slaves. 4. Indians civilized and savage. 1. The Portuguese are few in number, mostly married there, have lost sight of their native country, as well as the prospect of returning to it, and are disposed to become independant. 2. The native whites form the body of their nation. 3. The slaves are as numerous as the free. 4. The civilized Indians have no energy, and the savage would not meddle. . . .' The men of letters are those most desirous of a revolution. The people are not much under the influence of their priests, most of them read and write, possess arms, and are in the habit of using them for hunting. The slaves will take the side of their masters. In short, as to the question of revolution, there is but one mind in that country. But there appears no person capable of conducting a revolution, or willing to venture himself at it's head, without the aid of some powerful nation, as the people of their own might fail them. There is no printing press in Brasil. They consider the North American revolution as a precedent for theirs. They look to the United States as most likely to give them honest support, and from a variety of considerations have the strongest prejudices in our favor. . . . They would want cannon, ammunition, ships, sailors, souldiers and officers, for which they are disposed to look to the U.S., always understood that every service and furniture will be well paid. . . .

I took care to impress on him thro' the whole of our conversation that I had neither instructions nor authority to say a word to any body on this subject, and that I could only give him my own ideas as a single individual: which were that we were not in a condition at present to meddle nationally in any war; that we wished particularly to cultivate the friendship of Portugal, with whom we have an advan-

tageous commerce. That yet a succesful revolution in Brasil could not be uninteresting to us. . . .

I trouble Congress with these details, because, however distant we may be both in condition and dispositions, from taking an active part in any commotions in that country, nature has placed it too near us to make it's movements altogether indifferent to our interests or to our curiosity.

This rendezvous with the Brazilian, under such unlikely circumstances in such an unlikely place, proved to be the first of a long line of meetings with South American revolutionists seeking aid and comfort from North American revolutionists for their countries.

The south of France at the end of March was heaven to the sun-worshipping Virginian after the mists and cold and penetrating rains of Paris; in an exultant letter to Short he wrote:

I am now in the land of corn, wine, oil, and sunshine. What more can man ask of heaven? If I should happen to die at Paris I will beg of you to send me here, and have me exposed to the sun. I am sure it will bring me to life again. It is wonderful to me that every free being who possesses cent ecus de rente, does not remove to the Southward of the Loire. It is true that money will carry to Paris most of the good things of this canton. But it cannot carry thither it's sunshine, nor procure any equivalent for it.

Even the Provence tongue was a great delight.

I had thought the Provençale only a dialect of the French; on the contrary the French may rather be considered as a dialect of the Provençale. That is to say, the Latin is the original.

. . . It is my Italian which enables me to understand the people here, more than my French. This language, in different shades occupies all the country South of the Loire. Formerly it took precedence of the French under the name of la langue Romans. The ballads of it's Troubadours were the delight of the several courts of Europe, and it is from thence that the novels of the English are called Romances. Every letter is pronounced, the articulation is distinct, no nasal sounds disfigure it, and on the whole it stands close to the Italian and Spanish in point of beauty. I think it a general misfortune that historical circumstances gave a final prevalence to the French instead of the Provençale language.

To Lafayette, Jefferson explained from Nice what this trip to southern France meant to him. The journey "has been continued rapture to me," but it was more than a mere pleasure trip.

I am constantly roving about, to see what I have never seen before and shall never see again. In the great cities, I go to see what travellers think alone worthy of being seen; but I make a job of it, and generally gulp it all

The upper Po valley.

down in a day. On the other hand, I am never satiated with rambling through the fields and farms, examining the culture and cultivators, with a degree of curiosity which makes some take me to be a fool, and others to be much wiser than I am.

After giving a synopsis of his findings, his methods, and his motives, Jefferson invited the young general—now at the Assembly of Notables at Versailles, busily preparing himself to become a statesman—to join him to go about the country incognito, and learn something about his own country.

I have often wished for you. I think you have not made this journey. It is a pleasure you have to come, and an improvement to be added to the many you have already made. It will be a great comfort to you to know, from your own inspection, the condition of all the provinces of your own country, and it will be interesting to them at some future day to be known to you. This is perhaps the only moment of your life in which you can acquire that knolege. And to do it most effectually you must be absolutely incognito, you must ferret the people out of their hovels as I have done, look into their kettles, eat their bread, loll on their beds under pretence of resting yourself, but in fact to find if they are soft. You will feel a sublime pleasure in the course of this investigation, and a sublimer one hereafter when you shall be able to apply your knolege to the softening of their beds, or the throwing a morsel of meat into the kettle of vegetables.

Steps at Hyères.

This kind of advice—to come in contact with the common people and to take the trouble to discover their condition in order to ameliorate it—was entirely American, indeed entirely Jeffersonian, by nature. It must have sounded eccentric in the extreme to a Frenchman, particularly to a member of the aristocracy.

On April 6th Jefferson quit Marseilles for Italy—the seat of Rome, of classical culture, the home of poets and artists. But he was not going there for any of these reasons: he had heard that in the Piedmont they possessed a machine for cleaning rice which brought European rice to market less broken into fragments than American rice. In spite of his inquiries, no one who had seen the machine could intelligently describe or explain to Jefferson either its construction or how it worked. He wrote Short from Nice on April 12th:

At Marseilles they told me I should encounter the ricefeilds of Piedmont soon after

Colle di Tenda, the historic pass through the Alps between Nice and northern Italy.

crossing the Alps. Here they tell me there are none nearer than Vercelli and Novarra, which is carrying me almost to Milan. I fear that this circumstance will occasion me a greater delay than I had calculated on. However I am embarked in the project and shall go through with it. Tomorrow I set out on my passage over the Alps, being to pursue it 93 miles to Coni on mules, as the snows are not yet enough melted to admit carriages to pass. I leave mine here therefore, proposing to return by water from Genoa. I think it will be three weeks before I get back to Nice.

Passing through St. Raphael, La Napoule, Cannes, and Antibes to Nice and other scenic places of the Riviera as he made his way toward the mountain pass, he traveled through valleys "tolerably good," over mountains "always barren," on a road "generally near the sea, passing over little hills or strings of valleys." At Nice he found "this climate quite as superb as it has been represented." From there he left his carriage and headed north through the mountains by mule, crossing through a pass at the picturesque Colle di Tenda. Accustomed to the gentle scenery of his native Albe-

Old houses in the mountains near Limone.

Swollen streams feeding the Po River and Italian rice fields.

*The Maison Carrée at Nîmes. Jefferson wrote to his Parisian friend
Madame de Tessé in March 1787: "Here I am Madam, gazing whole hours
at the Maison quarrée, like a lover at his mistress. . . ."*

*Saorgio at the Colle di Tenda, where Jefferson made his passage
through the Alps. "Fall down and worship the site of the Chateau di Saorgio,"
he said; "you never saw, nor will ever see such another."*

marle County, he was hardly prepared for the breathtaking grandeur of the Alps:

Fall down and worship the site of the Chateau di Saorgio, you never saw, nor will ever see such another. The road is probably the greatest work of this kind which ever was executed either in antient or modern times. . . . Further on, we come to the Chateau di Saorgio, where a scene is presented, the most singular and picturesque I ever saw. The castle and village seem hanging to a cloud in front. On the right is a mountain cloven through to let pass a gurgling stream; on the left a river over which is thrown a magnificent bridge. The whole forms a bason, the sides of which are shagged with rocks, olive trees, vines, herds &c. . . . The produce along this passage is most generally olives except on the heights as before

observed, also corn, vines, mulberry, figs, cherries and walnuts. They have cows, goats and sheep. In passing on towards Tende, olives fail us ultimately at the village of Fontan, and there the chestnut trees begin in good quantity. Ciandola consists of only two houses, both taverns. Tende is a very inconsiderable village, in which they have not yet the luxury of glass windows: nor in any of the villages on this passage have they yet the fashion of powdering the hair. Common stone and limestone are so abundant that the apartments of every story are vaulted with stone to save wood.

The first Italian city of size which Jefferson visited was Turin, arriving on April 16th and staying for three days. From Turin he went slowly for the next two weeks through the rice country between Vercelli and Pavia; rice was

Rice fields between Vercelli and Novara.

Jefferson's hotel in Vercelli.

I examined another rice-beater of 6. pestles. They are 8 f[eet]. 9. I[nches]. long. Their ends, instead of being a truncated cone, have 9. teeth of iron, bound closely together. Each tooth is a double pyramid, joined at the base. When put together they stand [with] the upper ends placed in contact so as to form them into one great cone, and the lower end diverging. The upper are socketed into the end of the pestle, and the lower, when a little blunted by use, are not unlike the jaw-teeth of the Mammoth, with their studs. They say here that pestles armed with these teeth, clean the rice faster and break it less. The mortar too is of stone, which is supposed as good as wood, and more durable. One half of these pestles are always up. They rise about 21. I. Each makes 38. strokes in a minute. . . . The 6. pestles will clean 4000 lb. in 24 hours. The pound here is of 28. oz., the ounce equal to that of Paris. The best rice requires half an hour's boiling; a more indifferent kind somewhat less.

He wrote his old friend Edward Rutledge of Charleston about his pursuit of rice:

I set out from hence impressed with the idea the rice-dealers here had given me, that the difference between your rice and that of Piedmont proceeded from a difference in the machine for cleaning it. At Marseilles I hoped to know what the Piedmont machine was: but I could find nobody who knew any thing of it. I determined therefore to sift the matter to the bottom by crossing the Alps into the rice country. I found the machine exactly such a one as you had described to me in Congress in the year 1775. There was but one conclusion then to be drawn, to wit, that the rice was of a different species, and I determined to take enough to put you in seed: they informed me however that it's exportation in the husk was prohib-

to hold his attention throughout the whole of his journey on to Milan. He toured the fields, talked to the peasants and cultivators working the rice fields, and interviewed the owners. "The country continues plain and rich, the soil black," he noticed with admiration, and "is plentifully and beautifully watered at present." "From Vercelli to Novara the fields are all in rice, and now mostly under water." The rice machine, which he had traveled such a distance to see and finally found at Casino, aroused his diligent attention. It consisted of a beater arm with six pestles, each one serrated with teeth.

ited: so I could only bring off as much as my coat and surtout pockets would hold. I took measures with a muletier to run a couple of sacks across the Appenines to Genoa, but have not great dependance on it's success. The little therefore which I brought myself must be relied on for fear we should get no more; and because also it is genuine from Vercelli where the best is made of all the Sardinian Lombardy, the whole of which is considered as producing a better rice than the Milanese. This is assigned as the reason of the strict prohibition.

The return journey to Paris was arduous and took him to almost every section of France he had not yet visited. The most agreeable feature of it was a trip through the Canal du Midi, or Canal of Languedoc—a complicated waterway built by Louis XIV in the seventeenth century, which united the Mediterranean with the Atlantic. Jefferson became almost lyrical when describing this idyllic conclusion to his trip:

I have passed through the Canal from it's entrance into the mediterranean at Cette to this place, and shall be immediately at Toulouse, in the whole 200 American miles, by water; having employed in examining all it's details nine days, one of which was spent in making a tour of 40 miles on horseback, among the Montagnes noires, to see the manner in which water has been collected to supply the canal; the other eight on the canal itself. I dismounted my carriage from it's wheels, placed it on the deck of a light bark, and was thus towed on the canal instead of the post road. That I might be perfectly master of all the delays necessary, I hired a bark to myself by the day, and have made from 20. to 35 miles a day, according to circumstances, always sleeping ashore. Of all the methods of travel-

ling I have ever tried this is the pleasantest. I walk the greater part of the way along the banks of the canal, level, and lined with a double row of trees which furnish shade. When fatigued I take seat in my carriage where, as much at ease as if in my study, I read, write, or observe. My carriage being of glass all round, admits a full view of all the varying scenes thro' which I am shifted, olives, figs, mulberries, vines, corn and pasture, villages and farms. I have had some days of superb weather, enjoying two parts of the Indian's wish, cloudless skies and limpid waters: I have had another luxury which he could not wish, since we have driven him from the country of Mockingbirds, a double row of nightingales along the banks of the canal, in full song. This delicious bird gave me another rich treat at Vaucluse. Arriving there a little fatigued I sat down to repose myself at the fountain, which, in a retired hollow of the mountain, gushes out in a stream sufficient to

Branch of the Canal of Languedoc at Narbonne.

turn 300 mills, the ruins of Petrarch's chateau perched on a rock 200 feet perpendicular over the fountain, and every tree and bush filled with nightingales in full chorus. I find Mazzei's observation just that their song is more varied, their tone fuller and stronger here than on the banks of the Seine. It explains to me another circumstance, why there never was a poet North of the Alps, and why there never will be one. A poet is as much the creature of climate as an orange or palm tree. What a bird the nightingale would be in the climates of America! We must colonize him thither. You should not think of returning to America without taking the tour which I have taken, extending it only further South.

Citadel of Carcassonne on the Canal of Languedoc.

But there was a dark side to all of this too: all was not "cloudless skies and limpid waters." As he attempted to examine the construction and operation of the canal locks, as well as something about the navigation of the boats, he was repeatedly astonished and disgusted at the sight of the reversed working roles of the sexes in France: men did women's work, and women did men's. He commented on this at length in his notebook:

The locks are mostly kept by women, but the necessary operations are much too laborious for them. The encroachments by the men on the offices proper for the women is a great derangement in the order of things. Men are shoemakers, tailors, upholsterers, staymakers, mantua makers, cooks, door-keepers, housekeepers, housecleaners, bedmakers. They coëffe the ladies, and bring them to bed: the women therefore, to live are obliged to undertake the offices which they abandon. They become porters, carters, reapers, wood cutters, sailors, lock keepers, smiters on the anvil, cultivators of the earth &c. Can we wonder if such of them as have a little beauty prefer easier courses to get their livelihood, as long as that beauty lasts? Ladies who employ men in the offices which should be reserved for their sex, are they not bawds in effect? For every man whom they thus employ, some girl, whose place he has taken, is driven to whoredom.

Late in May, Jefferson came to Toulouse and the canal's end. He had been carried right through the heart of France. He continued on to Bordeaux, observing closely the culture of the famous white wines, and continued on to Nantes and Lorient to study the conditions in these seaports engaged in commerce with America. He arrived in Paris on June 10, 1787, after an absence of three months and ten days.

CHAPTER X

OBSERVER
OF REVOLUTION IN FRANCE
AND AMERICA (1787–1789)

*A*ND *now Jefferson was back in Paris. His return from his southern tour in 1787 coincided with two historic events of world-wide importance; on both sides of the Atlantic the world was stirring with revolutionary ferment. Both Europe and America were in turmoil, and Jefferson was compelled to shift the focus of his attention from one to the other with flexibility, rapidity, and a balanced point of view. He was a competent eyewitness of all that passed, from the Assembly of the Notables at Versailles in February 1787, called by a bewildered Louis XVI to advise him in the face of a financial situation of the greatest gravity, to the storming of the Bastille in July 1789. And he was a vigilant observer of the assembly of fifty-five Americans at Philadelphia, most of them lawyers and many of them known personally to him, gathered to draft a Constitution for the young American republic. In France* the ancien régime *was tottering on the brink of revolution. In Philadelphia the Federal Convention was in secret session debating the political future of the American nation.*

Jefferson watched the cruel misgovernment in Europe with fascination and keen intelligence. The oppressive conditions in France indicated to him an inevitable upheaval. He was tolerant of the dissatisfaction of the people; as he witnessed the edifice of tyranny beginning to crumble, he penned the most extreme statement he was ever to write on the subject of revolution in a letter to John Adams' son-in-law, Colonel William Stephens Smith. He advocated unequivocally the principle of rebellion.*

God forbid we should ever be 20. years without such a rebellion. The people can not be all, and always, well informed. The part which is wrong will be discontented in proportion to the importance of the facts they misconceive. If they remain quiet under such misconceptions it is a lethargy, the forerunner of death to the public liberty. We have had 13. states independant 11. years. There has been one rebellion. That comes to one rebellion in a century and a half for each state. What country before ever existed a century and half without a rebellion? And what country can preserve it's liberties if their rulers are not warned from time to time that their people preserve the spirit of resistance? Let them take arms. The remedy is to set them right as to facts, pardon and pacify them. What signify a few lives lost in a century or two? The tree of liberty must be refreshed from time to time with the blood of patriots and tyrants. It is it's natural manure.

Throughout his stay abroad, Jefferson was a critical observer of the desperate fate of the common man in the monarchical systems of the Old World: what he saw of "the vaunted scene of Europe" served only to deepen and intensify his democratic Americanism.

Amid the exciting circumstances and unfolding drama of the revolution in France, it was the events at home that engrossed Jefferson's attention most. It had long been realized by many sensible men—among them Jefferson—that the Articles of Confederation, under which the states had been acting in a loose confederacy, were unsatisfactory and inadequate for a solid and enduring union. Jefferson's experiences in Europe, particularly in the performance of his diplomatic functions in raising money and conducting foreign relations, had strengthened his desire for a complete reorganization of the government and for increasing national authority in matters of taxation, commerce, and foreign affairs. Jefferson felt and urged on his followers the necessity for a real union. "The politics of Europe render it indispensably necessary that with respect to everything external we be one nation only, firmly hooped together," he wrote Madison.

After sixteen weeks of strenuous work through the long summer months of 1787, and some inevitable compromise, the convention at Philadelphia finished its work. The secret deliberations were over and the great debate was ended; but as the final document was turned over to the states for ratification, a new debate erupted—this time in the open. The Constitution had been the product of many compromises, and both extremes denounced it: passions grew hot and parties emerged. During the crucial struggle over ways and means of insuring peace, justice, liberty, common defense, and general welfare, it was Jefferson's protégé—the black-clad, dry-humored, insignificant-looking Madison—who emerged as one of the great political minds of the proceedings. Jefferson had implicit confidence in Madison and in Washington, who had presided over the convention, but he was scarcely prepared for a change so sweeping as that embodied in the Constitution when it finally reached him in November.

His first reaction was decidedly mixed when he wrote Madison acknowledging receipt of his copy. There were a number of things he actually favored, as he read it, such as the creation of a strong government:

I like much the general idea of framing a government which should go on of itself peaceably, without needing continual recurrence to state legislatures. I like the organization of the government into Legislative, Judiciary and Executive. I like the power given the Legislature to levy taxes; and for that reason solely approve of the greater house being chosen by the people directly. For tho' I think a house chosen by them will be very illy qualified to legislate for the Union, for foreign nations &c. yet this evil does not weigh against the good of preserving inviolate the fundamental principle that the people are not to be taxed but by representatives chosen immediately by themselves. I am captivated by the compromise of the opposite claims of the great and little states, of the latter to equal, and the former to proportional influence. I am much pleased too with the substitution of the method of voting by persons, instead of that of voting by states: and I like the negative given to the Executive with a third of either house, though I should have liked it better had the Judiciary been associated for that purpose, or invested with a similar and separate power.

All that was excellent, as far as it went, but

Versailles.

it did not go far enough. He knew full well that a republican form of government was quite compatible with oppression, and he held with vehemence to the principle that the individual citizen is entitled to protection against misrule and intolerance. He believed that human liberties were at least as important as property rights; he had written these fundamentals of a democracy of free men into the preamble of the Declaration of Independence, but in reading the Constitution he found nothing specifically guaranteeing human rights and civil liberties. He objected first and foremost to the omission from the document of a bill of rights; to Madison he wrote:

I will now add what I do not like. First the omission of a bill of rights providing clearly and without the aid of sophisms for freedom of religion, freedom of the press, protection against standing armies, restriction against monopolies, the eternal and unremitting force of the habeas corpus laws, and trials by jury in all matters of fact triable by the laws of the land and not by the law of Nations. . . . Let me add that a bill of rights is what the people are entitled to against every government on earth, general or particular, and what no just government should refuse, or rest on inference.

Another thing he disliked most heartily about the Constitution was that it abandoned the principles of rotation in office and ineligibility for reelection: it put no time limit to officeholding. Jefferson favored a president elected for one term and ineligible forever after.

The second feature I dislike, and greatly dislike, is the abandonment in every instance of the necessity of rotation in office, and most particularly in the case of the President. Experience concurs with reason in concluding that the first magistrate will always be reelected if the constitution permits it. He is then an officer for life. . . . If once elected, and at a second or third election outvoted by one or two votes, he will pretend false votes, foul play, hold possession of the reins of government, be supported by the states voting for him, especially if they are the central ones lying in a compact body themselves and separating their opponents: and they will be aided by one nation of Europe, while the majority are aided by another. The election of a President of America some years hence will be much more interesting to certain nations of Europe than ever the election of a king of Poland was. . . . Experience shews that the only way to prevent disorder is to render [the elections] uninteresting by frequent changes.

These, then, were his two main objections to the Constitution: the lack of a bill of rights and the failure to prohibit reelection to office.

Another point the Constitution raised was the question of how much power the central government should have and exercise. This posed a painful dilemma for Jefferson. He knew that while strong governments have always been the enemies of the people, weak governments have never been able to protect them. To Madison he expressed himself on this problem:

I own I am not a friend to a very energetic government. It is always oppressive. The late rebellion in Massachusets has given more alarm than I think it should have done. Calculate that one rebellion in 13 states in the course of 11 years, is but one for each state in a century and a half. No country should be so long without one. Nor will any degree of power in the hands of government prevent insurrections.

The solution, he argued, lay in a balanced democracy, where public opinion should be free and enlightened and where the majority should prevail. There was a distinct possibility of going too far in the direction of a powerful government. "Our government wanted bracing," he admitted to Edward Rutledge. "Still we must take care not to run from one extreme to another; not to brace too high."

Jefferson found upon reflection and study of the Constitution that it "gained" on him. But one objection remained and rankled him: there was still no bill of rights. With ever-increasing fervor and determination he pressed his demand for its incorporation. Finally a proposal of Massachusetts was carried, with Jefferson's approval, that the Constitution should be adopted as it stood and that amendments should follow. Otherwise, the whole Constitution might have been endangered if it were referred back to a new convention. And eventually the matter of the bill of rights was safely and legally rectified by appropriate amendments.

In the heated debate surrounding ratification of the Constitution by the states, factions and political parties developed. In the sense that he favored a strong federal union, Jefferson was as much a "federalist" by temperament as Madison. He looked with grave misgivings on Antifederalists in his own state, where a man like Patrick Henry, who opposed ratification, had the influence and power to engineer Madison's defeat to the Senate. But as the Federalists emerged as a political party and were elected to Congress, he found him-

*self arrayed in principle against the funda-
mental tenets of a group of men who were
themselves against the form of democracy
which he favored. He soon learned the jarring
truth of this, when Francis Hopkinson wrote
him that he had heard Jefferson was an "anti-
federalist." He replied frankly, stating his political philosophy and drawing a distinction
between federalism and the Federalist political party.*

You say that I have been dished up to you as
an antifederalist, and ask me if it be just. My
opinion was never worthy enough of notice to
merit citing: but since you ask it I will tell it
you. I am not a Federalist, because I never submitted the whole system of my opinions to the
creed of any party of men whatever in religion,
in philosophy, in politics, or in any thing else
where I was capable of thinking for myself.
Such an addiction is the last degradation of a
free and moral agent. If I could not go to
heaven but with a party, I would not go there
at all. Therefore I protest to you I am not of
the party of federalists. But I am much farther
from that of the Antifederalists. I approved
from the first moment, of the great mass of
what is in the new constitution, the consolida-
tion of the government, the organisation into
Executive, legislative and judiciary, the subdi-
vision of the legislative, the happy compromise
of interests between the great and little states
by the different manner of voting in the different houses, the voting by persons instead of
states, the qualified negative on laws given to
the Executive which however I should have
liked better if associated with the judiciary also as in New York, and the power of taxation.
I thought at first that the latter might have
been limited. A little reflection soon convinced
me it ought not to be. What I disapproved from
the first moment also was the want of a bill of

rights to guard liberty against the legislative
as well as executive branches of the government, that is to say to secure freedom in religion, freedom of the press, freedom from monopolies, freedom from unlawful imprisonment, freedom from a permanent military, and
a trial by jury in all cases determinable by the
laws of the land. I disapproved also the perpetual reeligibility of the President. To these
points of disapprobation I adhere.

*Later, the Federalists were to clamor about
the infamy and divisiveness of parties—except
their own—calling them "factions," after Jefferson organized and became the head of his
own political party in order to combat the anti-
democratic views of the Federalists.*

*Jefferson's final reaction to the Constitution
was enthusiastic, especially after the Bill of
Rights was attached to it. He wrote David
Humphreys from Paris in March 1789:*

The operations which have taken place in
America lately, fill me with pleasure. In the
first place they realize the confidence I had that
whenever our affairs get obviously wrong, the
good sense of the people will interpose and set
them to rights. The example of changing a
constitution by assembling the wise men of the
state, instead of assembling armies, will be
worth as much to the world as the former examples we had given them. The constitution
too which was the result of our deliberations,
is unquestionably the wisest ever yet presented
to men, and some of the accomodations of interest which it has adopted are greatly pleasing to me who have before had occasions of seeing how difficult those interests were to accomodate.

*In the meantime the temper of the people in
France was rising dangerously as the country*

was rapidly disintegrating and moving toward a series of tremendous cataclysms. The people were frightened with the exposure of the financial plight of the nation, with the public credit affected and the nation moving headlong toward bankruptcy, and "such a spirit of discontent," he wrote Monroe, "as has never been seen." He watched the spectacle unfolding before him with hope and fear, sharing in the ardent democratic hopes of his patriot friends and at the same time dreading the undeterminable consequences of violence. In August 1787 he wrote Washington that "the discovery of the abominable abuses of public money by the late comptroller general, some new expences of the court, not of a peice with the projects of reformation, and the imposition of new taxes, have in the course of a few weeks raised a spirit of discontent in this nation, so great and so general, as to threaten serious consequences."

Jefferson followed the development of the upheaval with attentive, passionate interest from its first murmurings until the very day of his departure. Throughout this gigantic struggle he clung to the belief that out of the struggle would come reforms without the uprooting of the monarchy. France had far too old a history and political institutions far too deeply rooted to consider sweeping them out of existence.

It was known to be impossible for the king to be able to impose new taxes to shore up the exhausted public credit; the only resource left to the king and his ministers was to appeal to the nation to grant money to the government if they would consent to reforms so long overdue. Yet Jefferson's optimism for the future of France persisted through the fall of 1788. By January 1789 he was able to write Dr. Richard Price with an uncanny insight into political drifts of the process that was leading to the nascent revolution:

You say you are not sufficiently informed about the nature and circumstances of the present struggle here. Having been on the spot from it's first origin and watched it's movements as an uninterested spectator, with no other bias than a love of mankind I will give you my ideas of it. Tho' celebrated writers of this and other countries had already sketched good principles on the subject of government, yet the American war seems first to have awakened the thinking part of this nation in general from the sleep of despotism in which they were sunk. The officers too, who had been to America, were mostly young men, less shackled by habit and prejudice, and more ready to assent to the dictates of common sense and common right. They came back impressed with these. The press, notwithstanding it's shackles, began to disseminate them: conversation too assumed new freedoms; politics became the theme of all societies, male and female, and a very extensive and zealous party was formed, which may be called the Patriotic party, who sensible of the abusive government under which they lived, longed for occasions of reforming it. This party comprehended all the honesty of the kingdom, sufficiently at it's leisure to think: the men of letters, the easy bourgeois, the young nobility, partly from reflection partly from mode; for those sentiments became a matter of mode, and as such united most of the young women to the party.

The revolutionary fever rose rapidly in France in the spring of 1789 after incredible bungling, confusion, and debt-piling on the part of the bewildered monarch. Louis XVI, who was a despot in law but a weakling in practice, had been forced to resort to what was, for him, the humiliating process of consulting with the representatives of the people. The king and his ministers were slow in carry-

Fontainebleau, the château in the forest: "The king comes here in the fall always, to hunt."

ing out reform measures, which in turn resulted in *"new claims to be advanced, and a pressure to arise for a fixed constitution, not subject to changes at the will of the King."*

After the opening of the Estates General in the beginning of May, Jefferson went daily from Paris to Versailles and attended their debates; he observed that *"had it been enlightened with lamps and chandeliers, it would have been almost as brilliant as the opera."* He told of the oath of the Commons delegates that they would never separate of their own accord until they had settled a national constitution, of the revolt of the aristocracy, of the vacillation of the king, and of Necker's offer to resign as minister of finance.

The Noblesse were in triumph; the people in consternation. I was quite alarmed at this state of things. The soldiery had not yet indicated which side they should take, and that which they should support would be sure to prevail. I considered a successful reformation of government in France, as ensuring a gen-

The library of Louis XVI at Versailles.

eral reformation thro Europe, and the resurrection, to a new life, of their people, now ground to dust by the abuses of the governing powers. I was much acquainted with the leading patriots of the assembly. Being from a country which had successfully passed thro' a similar reformation, they were disposed to my acquaintance, and had some confidence in me. I urged most strenuously an immediate compromise; to secure what the government was now ready to yield, and trust to future occasions for what might still be wanting.

Among the members of the Estates General, particularly among the liberals, Jefferson had many friends who were preparing to clip the wings of absolutism. Jefferson himself was not an extremist and constantly urged moderation upon the fiery Patriots, advising them to avoid violence, to compromise with the king, and to buy him off with financial concessions in return for political liberties.

Events moved with dramatic swiftness through the early summer. The Third Estate, representing the common people, withdrew

Council chambers of Louis XVI at Fontainebleau.

from the Estates General on June 17th and took the bold and revolutionary step of calling itself the National Assembly, and began to consider the state of the country and to legislate. Desperate confusion reigned. Jefferson wrote Madison on June 18th:

The Commons have in their chamber almost all the talents of the nation; they are firm and bold, yet moderate. There is indeed among them a number of very hot headed members; but those of most influence are cool, temperate, and sagacious. Every step of this house has been marked with caution and wisdom. The Noblesse on the contrary are absolutely out of their senses. They are so furious they can seldom debate at all.

The Third Estate, by a series of bold enactments, was attempting to transfer jurisdiction over finances to itself. On a memorable June 20th the deputies found themselves locked out of their chambers and further sessions were suspended on royal order. They assembled at a nearby indoor tennis court at Versailles and swore to the "Tennis Court Oath," a solemn compact never to separate until a constitution had been granted by the king. The real Revolution had begun: on July 14th a crowd of angry Parisians, having seized arms, stormed the massive-stoned Bastille and killed its governor.

Paris and Versailles seethed with excitement as the Revolution spread like wildfire among the other two estates—nobility and clergy—which melted under the intense heat into the National Assembly. And the Assembly, sensing its growing strength, began to demand boldly a share in the government of France from the king. The conflict over the constitution split the ranks of the National Assembly, and some of the abler members decided to talk over the situation in a calm at-

mosphere. Lafayette wrote Jefferson in late August asking him for permission to bring six or eight members of the Assembly for dinner. Thus it happened that Jefferson became involved with certain members of the Assembly in an incident that, as he said, had the most far-reaching consequences.

When they arrived, they were La Fayette himself, Duport, Barnave, Alexander La Meth, Blacon, Mounier, Maubourg, and Dagout. These were leading patriots, of honest but differing opinions sensible of the necessity of effecting a coaliton by mutual sacrifices, knowing each other, and not afraid therefore to unbosom themselves mutually. This last was a material principle in the selection. With this view the Marquis had invited the conference and had fixed the time & place inadvertently as to the embarrassment under which it might place me. The cloth being removed and wine set on the table, after the American manner, the Marquis introduced the objects of the conference by summarily reminding them of the state of things in the Assembly, the course which the principles of the constitution were taking, and the inevitable result, unless checked by more concord among the Patriots themselves. He observed that altho' he also had his opinion, he was ready to sacrifice it to that of his brethren of the same cause: but that a common opinion must now be formed, or the Aristocracy would carry everything, and that whatever they should now agree on, he, at the head of the National force, would maintain. The discussions began at the hour of four, and were continued till ten o'clock in the evening; during which time I was a silent witness to a coolness and candor of argument unusual in the conflicts of political opinion; to a logical reasoning, and chaste eloquence, disfigured by no gaudy tinsel of rhetoric or declamation, and

The boudoir redecorated for Marie Antoinette at Fontainebleau.

truly worthy of being placed in parallel with the finest dialogues of antiquity, as handed to us by Xenophon, by Plato and Cicero. The result was an agreement that the king should have a suspensive veto on the laws, that the legislature should be composed of a single body only, & that to be chosen by the people. This Concordate decided the fate of the constitution. The Patriots all rallied to the principles thus settled, carried every question agreeably to them, and reduced the Aristocracy to insignificance and impotence. But duties of exculpation were now incumbent on me. I waited on Count Montmorin the next morning, and explained to him with truth and candor how it had happened that my house had been made the scene of conferences of such a character. He told me he already knew everything which had passed, that, so far from taking umbrage at the use made of my house on that occasion, he earnestly wished I would habitually assist at such conferences, being sure I should be useful in moderating the warmer spirits, and promoting a wholesome and practicable reformation only.

This was Jefferson's last personal involvement with the French Revolution.

For over a year Jefferson had been asking Congress for leave to return to America for a few months in order to take his daughters home, for he felt they needed the "society & care of their friends" in America now that they were growing up. Then he planned to return to France. Now that Washington had been inaugurated as the chief executive, he wrote him:

In a letter to Mr. Jay of the 19. of November I asked a leave of absence to carry my children back to their own country, and to settle various matters of a private nature which were left unsettled because I had no idea of being absent so long. . . . I am excessively anxious to receive the permission without delay, that I may be able to get back before the winter sets in. Nothing can be so dreadful to me as to be shivering at sea for two or three months in a winter passage.

Washington promptly complied with his request. Jefferson received the news at the end of August 1789 and left Paris in the latter part of September, believing he would be returning to his post within a few months. Years later when he came to write his Autobiography, *he paid a touching tribute to the country where he had spent five rich and fruitful years. His faith in the ultimate benefit of the French Revolution to humanity was never shaken.*

And here I cannot leave this great and good country without expressing my sense of it's preeminence of character among the nations of the earth. A more benevolent people, I have never known, nor greater warmth & devotedness in their select friendships. Their kindness and accommodation to strangers is unparalleled, and the hospitality of Paris is beyond anything I had conceived to be practicable in a large city. Their eminence too in science, the communicative dispositions of their scientific men, the politeness of the general manners, the ease and vivacity of their conversation, give a charm to their society to be found nowhere else. In a comparison of this with other countries we have the proof of primacy, which was given to Themistocles after the battle of Salamis. Every general voted to himself the first reward of valor, and the second to Themistocles. So ask the travelled inhabitant of any nation, In what country on earth would you rather live?—Certainly in my own, where are all my friends, my relations, and the earliest & sweetest affections and recollections of my life. Which would be your second choice? France.

Never was a more noble tribute paid to this noble nation.

On September 26, 1789, Jefferson with Polly and Patsy started out from Paris for LeHavre, to sail first to England and then home. The voyage was accompanied by favoring winds and fine weather, and after a smooth passage of one month the Jeffersons set foot on American soil again at Norfolk on November 23, 1789. Never again was Jefferson to leave his native country.

Canal of Languedoc or Canal du Midi across France, a complicated waterway uniting the Mediterranean with the Atlantic Ocean, through which Jefferson returned to Paris from his tour of southern France.

*The Natural Bridge, located on Jefferson's own property in
Rockbridge County, Virginia, which he described in his
Notes on the State of Virginia as "the most sublime of Nature's works."*

CHAPTER XI

SECRETARY
OF STATE (1790-1793)

As soon as the ship reached Norfolk, Jefferson promptly set out for Richmond and Monticello with his daughters, stopping however on the way at Eppington, the residence of their relatives the Eppeses. There an express courier brought to Jefferson a letter from President Washington offering him the post of secretary of state in the newly formed Cabinet. The punctilious Washington emphasized that he had no desire to interfere with Jefferson's desires, but he tactfully hinted that he would very much appreciate having him in his Cabinet.

It was a flattering offer and Jefferson was not insensible to it. Washington, for whom he had the greatest respect, was in a difficult position, needing all the help he could get: this was the first consideration. "The federal business has proceeded with a mortifying tardiness," his friend Madison had informed him while he was still in France. "We are in a wilderness without a single footstep to guide us." But all the same Jefferson was confronted with a dilemma as he pondered the offer of another political job, which meant more years of sacrifice, of mounting personal debt, of bitter criticism, and of separation from his family. Washington "kindly leaves it optional in me to accept of that or remain at Paris as I chuse," he wrote Short the day before answering Washington's letter. "It is impossible to give a flat refusal to such a nomination." After weighing the offer several days, he informed the president that, while he preferred to return to his post in Paris, he would accept the appointment of secretary of state in the new government if Washington believed it was best for the public welfare. Washington did insist and on February 14, 1790, Jefferson informed him that he would "no longer hesitate to undertake the office to which you are pleased to call me."

Having left the decision in the hands of the president, Jefferson's mind was relieved and he continued with eagerness and obvious joy to Monticello, where he lingered through January and February 1790 to place his private affairs in order. He was more popular than ever in his native state; a committee of his old Albemarle constituents called on him with an address of congratulation. What gladdened his heart more than anything else was the approaching marriage of his eldest daughter, Martha (called Patsy), to young Thomas Mann Randolph Jr., the eldest son of Colonel Randolph of Tuckahoe and a second cousin. They had known each other as children and had seen something of each other during the summer of 1788 in Paris when he came to pay his respects while studying at the University of Edinburgh. Jefferson was overjoyed with the match. The arrangements were concluded between the paternal parents—both mothers were dead—and the wedding took place at Monticello on February 23rd.

Music corner in the parlor at Monticello, with piano bought in England and music rack probably made locally.

"My daughter is married agreeably to my most sanguine wishes," he wrote a friend in Paris. "The talents, temper, family and fortune of the young gentleman are all I could have desired." They were a distinguished pair. John Randolph once described Jefferson's daughter as "the noblest woman in Virginia," and Jefferson had the highest praise for his son-in-law in his Autobiography: "a young gentleman of genius, science and honorable mind, who afterwards filled a dignified station in the General Government, & the most

dignified in his own State." With the affairs of his farms placed in reasonable order and his daughter safely married, he left Monticello by phaeton on March 1, 1790, bound for New York to assume the newly created office of secretary of state.

Congress was in session and, after being cordially received by the president, he plunged at once into foreign and domestic problems that had been accumulating for months. All of his young colleagues had already taken charge of their respective departments: the *thirty-three-year-old Alexander Hamilton in the treasury; the forty-year-old Henry Knox in the war department; and the forty-three-year-old Edmund Randolph, a fellow Virginian, was attorney general. None were strangers to him. Jefferson himself was only a month short of his forty-seventh birthday when he assumed his duties as secretary of state.*

Jefferson found to his consternation in returning to America that a kind of weariness and cynicism had set in, that the tyrannical system of England was now admired and emulated, while the rising revolutionary spirit of France was feared and dreaded. Something had happened to America in his absence; the very principles of the Revolution were beginning to erode as Hamilton and his friends worked in sinister ways to establish English-like institutions, such as a monarchy and aristocracy, in this country. Fresh from witnessing the initial stages of the French Revolution, he was now back in America with his republican ideals newly burnished:

Here certainly I found a state of things which, of all I had ever contemplated, I the least expected. I had left France in the first year of its revolution, in the fervor of natural rights, and zeal for reformation. My conscientious devotion to these rights could not be heightened, but it had been aroused and excited by daily exercise.

The man with whom Jefferson clashed almost immediately was the arch financier of the United States, Alexander Hamilton. When the secretary of state confronted the aggressive, eloquent, vigorous, brilliantly opinionated secretary of the treasury—an exponent of a strong, centralized government—their sharply divergent points of view soon erupted violently into a conflict of epic proportions. A foreigner of obscure origin and illegitimate birth—"the bastard brat of a Scots pedlar," as blunt-spoken John Adams testily called him—he climbed to the top by sheer force of will and superior genius. Hamilton was not the kind of man Jefferson could like or understand. Men, Hamilton was convinced, were governed and could be moved only by crude self-interest and force; he fearlessly accepted the corollary that corruption is an indispensable instrument of government.

Hamilton's general plan for safeguarding the republic from "the imprudence of democracy" was that of consolidating the interests of certain broad classes of "the rich and well-born" with the interests of the government. Hamilton, unlike Jefferson, was not interested in liberty; he was concerned with property and the national debt. His first move was for funding all the obligations of the government at face value, thereby putting the interests of the speculator on a par with those of the original holder of the government's securities. There remained the question of the debts incurred by the several states during the course of the war; the reorganization plan that Hamilton proposed was outlined in his famous "assumption" by which the federal government would "assume" the states' debts, with a discount to be determined, through some sort of central organization. The opponents of the measure, particularly from the southern states where the population was comparatively smaller, objected strenuously to the federal measures for raising additional revenue. When Jefferson arrived in New York to take possession of his office, the debate over funding and assumption was at its height.

Hamilton's financial system had then past. It had two objects. 1st as a puzzle, to exclude popular understanding & inquiry. 2dly, as a

machine for the corruption of the legislature; for he avowed the opinion that man could be governed by one of two motives only, force or interest: force he observed, in this country, was out of the question; and the interests therefore of the members must be laid hold of, to keep the legislature in unison with the Executive. And with grief and shame it must be acknoleged that his machine was not without effect. That even in this, the birth of our government, some members were found sordid enough to bend their duty to their interests, and to look after personal, rather than public good. . . . Immense sums were thus filched from the poor & ignorant, and fortunes accumulated by those who had themselves been poor enough before. Men thus enriched by the dexterity of a leader, would follow of course the chief who was leading them to fortune, and become the zealous instruments of all his enterprises. This game was over, and another was on the carpet at the moment of my arrival; and to this I was most ignorantly & innocently made to hold the candle. This fiscal maneuvre is well known by the name of the Assumption. . . .

The quid pro quo *of effecting assumption came through a bargain that was struck between Hamilton and two Virginia congressmen at Jefferson's dinner table: the Virginians gave their word to switch their votes in favor of assumption and Hamilton promised he would get enough northern members of Congress to vote for the bill establishing the location of the national capital at Georgetown on the Potomac in ten years' time. Years later Jefferson called his part in this trade-and-deal the greatest political blunder of his life.*

He simply did not foresee the end result of Hamilton's plan: namely, a conflict over what economic interests would eventually con-

trol the government of the United States. An almost irreconcilable difference of opinion, therefore, sprang up between Hamilton and Jefferson on nearly every major issue to come before Washington's Cabinet. Their sharply divergent points of view, and the key positions they occupied in these formative years of the republic, lifted their struggle from the level of politics to the realm of fundamental doctrines. Jefferson could hardly conceal his contempt for this upstart who made himself the spokesman of the commercial-financial interests. While serving in the Cabinet, the two men did maintain social contact, but the deep current of antipathy between them was difficult to suppress.

Jefferson never became accustomed to political conflict and never did thrive in an atmosphere of suspicion and opposition. It was conviction, not inclination, that dragged him into open conflict with the secretary of the treasury and the Federalists. Under Hamilton's aggressive leadership, financiers and speculators—"stockjobbers" as Jefferson called them—were getting a grip upon the federal government. Hamilton's financial policies, with his funding, excise, assumption, and bank bills, were taking effect. Jefferson was filled with dismay as he watched the democratic republic, which he envisioned as a commonwealth inhabited by men who tilled the fields, becoming "corrupt" and falling into the hands of merchants, financiers, and speculators who were flourishing and making money. Successful and powerful, Hamilton became inevitably the head of this powerful group of "special interests"—success increased his power and power swelled his bumptiousness. More and more the secretary of the treasury meddled in matters that were not strictly his concern. At Cabinet meetings the aggressive Hamilton spoke his mind with fervor and

Saint Paul's Chapel, New York, where it is believed Jefferson attended services with President Washington.

stated his opinions with arrogance. As his contempt for democracy grew, so did his disregard for the secretary of state.

Jefferson grew increasingly unhappy in New York, and the strain of the struggle became so great that his health began to suffer. His severe headaches, probably a symptom of nervous tension, began to reoccur. He had many hours of unhappiness and moments of doubt; when he wrote his son-in-law Thomas Mann Randolph, inquiring about the trees and crops at Monticello, he concluded with desperate sincerity: "I long to be free for pursuits of this kind instead of the detestable ones in which I am now labouring without pleasure to myself or profit to others." Why was he wasting his time in the abrasive disputes of politics, when he could be home cultivating his lands and living with his family? He sincerely wished to escape forever from public affairs.

What added immensely to his disgust with Philadelphia and public life in 1791 was the sudden explosion of a personal dispute which threatened to endanger his "antient friendship" with John Adams. Thomas Paine had published his famous pamphlet on The Rights of Man *in England, which was a bold defense of the French Revolution and its principles. When copies reached America in the spring of 1791, Madison loaned one to Jefferson; when the owner of the pamphlet requested that it be returned, for it was the only copy at his disposal and he intended to have it reprinted in Philadelphia, Jefferson courteously returned it with an innocuous note in which he expressed his satisfaction that such a valuable work would appear in America:*

I am extremely pleased to find it will be reprinted here, and that something is at length to be publicly said against the political heresies which have sprung up among us. I have no doubt our citizens will rally a second time round the standard of 'Common Sense.'

Jefferson was thunderstruck to find that the enterprising publisher, without asking his permission, issued the American edition of The Rights of Man *with these words of approval from the secretary of state publicly and prominently displayed on the cover. He saw at once that this unauthorized publication of his letter would create a tremendous storm. The words "political heresies" could only apply to Federalists, and among the Federalists to John Adams in particular, whose "Discourses on Davila" had been appearing in John Fenno's* Gazette of the United States. *Adams had scented the dangers to society in French republicanism and had recently given expression to a reasoned, philosophical statement of oligarchical principles of government. Jefferson was sincerely mortified by the printer's indiscretion and declared that nothing was further from his intentions than to appear as a contradictor of Adams in public. Finally Jefferson wrote the injured sage to explain that he never intended or wished to appear on the public stage as an antagonist of his theories of government:*

I have a dozen times taken up my pen to write to you and as often laid it down again, suspended between opposing considerations. I determine however to write from a conviction that truth, between candid minds, can never do harm. . . . That you and I differ in our ideas of the best form of government is well known to us both: but we have differed as friends should do, respecting the purity of each other's motives, and confining our difference of opinion to private conversation. And I can declare with truth in the presence of the almighty that nothing was further from my intention or expectation than to have had either my own or your name brought before the public on this occasion. The friendship and confidence which has so long existed between us required this explanation from me, and I know you too well to fear any misconstruction of the motives of it.

Adams accepted the explanation more gracefully than was to be expected, but objected to Jefferson's statement concerning their differences in philosophy: "I know not what your Idea is of the best form of Government. You and I have never had a serious conversation together that I can recollect concerning the nature of Government. The very transient hints that have ever passed between Us have been jocular and superficial, without ever coming to any explanation. If You suppose that I have or ever had a design or desire, of attempting to introduce a Government of King, Lords and Commons, or in other Words an hereditary Executive, or an hereditary Senate, either into the Government of the United States or that of any Individual State, in this Country, you are wholly mistaken."

Ever since their return from Europe, the two old friends had gradually diverged in political philosophy, and the intimacy of former days, though not completely gone, had nevertheless suffered considerable damage.

Before long, another storm burst round Jefferson's head. The Northern-commercial interests led by Hamilton had for some time had an effective mouthpiece in gaining wide support through Fenno's Gazette of the United States; *the partisan paper had been used to trumpet the views of the Federalists and to castigate the Southern-agrarian group led by Jefferson. The pernicious propaganda, unrestrained utterances, and abusive tone of Fenno's newspaper angered Jefferson and made him realize that*

The First Bank of the United States, Philadelphia.

the Republicans were poorly armed without their own paper to express their views and counteract these attacks. As a result Jefferson brought Philip Freneau, the poet journalist and ardent democrat, into his office and eight months later in October helped him launch the National Gazette, *with Freneau as editor. Freneau's pen was mordant and savage, attacking with reckless abandon Hamilton, Adams, the Federalists in Congress, the evils of paper money and speculation, the Bank Bill, Hamilton's report on manufactures, monarchists, and aristocrats, and even the noble Washington by indirection at times. The sud-*

den appearance of this new and powerful anti-Federalist newspaper, edited by the newly appointed clerk for foreign languages working in Jefferson's office, raised an angry outcry. Hamilton, the particular target, was personally wounded by the ridicule and barbs of Freneau. Hamilton's editor, Fenno, replied in defense by resorting to name-calling. Despite the conspicuous silence of the publicity-shy Jefferson, the press war increased in virulence and ferocity.

The open secret of the dissensions behind the impressive façade of the Washington administration became a public sensation. President Washington, a man of moderation and prudence, was mortified by these violent attacks and passionate outbursts within his Cabinet printed in the warring gazettes. The feud threatened the republic with disunity. He was tired of politics and did not want to run again for office in 1792; both Jefferson and Hamilton realized that there was no one of sufficient political stature to replace Washington and pleaded with him to be a candidate for a second term. An unalterable sense of duty in the end made Washington agree to run for office a second time in order to preserve the unity of the nation. But at the end of August he made a sharp appeal to both men for moderation. He expressed his distress at the dissensions that had taken place within the government when "we are encompassed on all sides with avowed enemies." To both men he repeated the phrase that was uppermost in his mind; he asked that "there may be liberal allowances, mutual forbearances, and temporizing yieldings on all sides." Jefferson was in Virginia when Washington's oblique rebuke reached him. Stung by the implied criticism, he made a vigorous defense of his position and went thoroughly into his differences with Hamilton in a letter, dated September 9th, of nearly three thousand

words. He wrote later with resentment of his part in Hamilton's Assumption Bill:

I was duped . . . by the Secretary of the Treasury and made a tool for forwarding his schemes, not then sufficiently understood by me; and of all the errors of my political life, this has occasioned me the deepest regret.

He denounced Hamilton for his conspiratorial attempts to corrupt Congress and thereby to destroy freedom, and he accused him of interfering in his own State Department and sabotaging foreign policy. On the question of Freneau, he emphatically denied that he had influenced him or written for his paper, even though he was a supporter of the editor, whose ideas he shared and whose genius he appreciated. He concluded by expressing his desire to retire from public office at the end of the administration, and warned Washington that as a private citizen he would consider himself free to defend himself publicly against Hamilton's slanders:

When I came into this office, it was with a resolution to retire from it as soon as I could with decency. It pretty early appeared to me that the proper moment would be the first of those epochs at which the constitution seems to have contemplated a periodical change or renewal of the public servants. In this I was confirmed by your resolution respecting the same period; from which however I am happy in hoping you have departed. I look to that period with the longing of a wave-worn mariner, who has at length the land in view, & shall count the days & hours which still lie between me & it. . . . I will not suffer my retirement to be clouded by the slanders of a man whose history, from the moment at which history can stoop to notice him, is a tissue of machinations against the liberty of the country which has not only received and given him bread, but heaped it's honors on his head.

Five days after he wrote this letter, Jefferson started back to Philadelphia and stopped on the way at Mount Vernon to call on Washington; only after much earnest conversation was Washington able to dissuade him, at least temporarily, from resignation. But the matter was too deep-seated and the cleavage too fundamental for any permanent compromise to be reached.

In the autumn of 1792, in an atmosphere of intense political bitterness, Washington reluctantly stood for reelection and received the unanimous vote of the Electoral College. Adams was also reelected in spite of a strong vote against him. But the election was most significant because of the emergence of Jefferson's own party, the Republican, as a political power of national importance by gaining control of the House of Representatives. In a sense, the 1792 campaign was a projection of the Jefferson-Hamilton conflict onto the national arena.

It had been Jefferson's purpose for nearly two years to retire from public life. At first, he had set the date at the end of Washington's first term, but at each suggestion of his purpose to withdraw, Washington, by pleading considerations of the public good as well as his own personal desires, prevailed upon him to remain. Finally, Jefferson's resolution to resign was strengthened by the unpleasant task of having to demand the recall of the explosive and high-handed "Citizen" Genêt, the minister of the French Republic, who had made a disingenuous attempt to embroil Washington with Congress and the whole administration with the people. Jefferson had reluctantly

consented earlier to continue to serve in the Cabinet, until the Freneau matter, with the personal bitterness it engendered, confirmed Jefferson's distaste for a position which called for daily contest with an aggressive and untiring opponent.

On July 21, 1793, Jefferson again tendered his resignation to Washington, to take effect the end of September. He intended to retire from those scenes for "which I am every day more & more convinced that neither my talents, tone of mind, nor time of life fit me." Washington was dismayed to receive Jefferson's formal note of resignation. His Cabinet was crumbling around him, for Hamilton had also expressed a similar determination to retire. He therefore personally called on Jefferson to dissuade him; with reluctance Jefferson agreed to continue as secretary of state through December.

No stronger summary of Jefferson's service in the Cabinet can be given than Washington's stately and gracious letter of regret over his resignation: "Since it has been impossible to prevail upon you to forego any longer the indulgence of your desire for private life, the event, however anxious I am to avert it, must be submitted to. But I cannot suffer you to leave your station without assuring you that the opinion which I have formed of your integrity and talents, and which dictated your original nomination, has been confirmed by the fullest experience, and that both have been displayed in the discharge of your duty. Let a conviction of my most earnest prayers for your happiness accompany you in your retirement."

On January 5, 1794, Jefferson said farewell to his friends and colleagues, leaving Philadelphia and the public affairs and squabble of politics—to the best of his knowledge and belief—forever.

CHAPTER XII

RURAL INTERLUDE AT MONTICELLO
(1794–1797)

WHEN *Jefferson left Philadelphia in January 1794, he felt weary and already old beyond his years. As far as he knew, he was leaving politics forever and going home to become a family patriarch and a gentleman farmer. He was sick of the drudgeries of office and of the steady contention with Hamilton, and he was in earnest about retiring from active politics. To his South Carolina friend and colleague in the Continental Congress, Edward Rutledge, he wrote:*

I had retired after five & twenty years of constant occupation in public affairs, and total abandonment of my own. I retired much poorer than when I entered the public service, and desired nothing but rest & oblivion.

On January 16th he climbed the winding road to Monticello, the peaceful retreat where he would be sheltered from further storms.

During the last three years he had taken a rough beating at the hands of Hamilton and the Federalist newspapers, and he came home with deep scars and distasteful memories. Weary and hurt and in urgent need of a complete rest and agricultural quietude, he plunged into farming with a zeal he had never known before, and he did not mind letting his friends in Philadelphia know he did not miss the political snipings and party intrigues of their work.

I return to farming with an ardour which I scarcely knew in my youth, and which has got the better entirely of my love of study. Instead of writing 10. or 12. letters a day, which I have been in the habit of doing as a thing of course, I put off answering my letters now, farmerlike, till a rainy day, and then find it sometimes postponed by other necessary occupations.

Several years later he reiterated his deeply entrenched feelings to Adams about political life: "I have no ambition to govern men. It is a painful and thankless office."

When the Duc de la Rochefoucauld-Liancourt visited Monticello in 1796, he noticed and recorded the progress Jefferson had made in his work on the building: "The house stands on the summit of the mountain, and the taste and arts of Europe have been consulted in the formation of its plan. Mr. Jefferson had commenced its construction before the American revolution; since that epocha his life has been constantly engaged in public affairs, and he has not been able to complete the execution of

Monticello from Brown's Mountain.

the whole extent of the project which it seems he had at first conceived. That part of the building which was finished has suffered from the suspension of the work, and Mr. Jefferson, who two years since resumed the habits and leisure of private life, is now employed in repairing the damage occasioned by this interruption, and still more by his absence; he continues his original plan, and even improves on it, by giving to his buildings more elevation and extent. He intends that they should consist only of one story, crowned with balustrades; and a dome is to be constructed in the center of the structure. The apartments will be large and convenient; the decoration, both outside and inside, simple, yet regular and elegant. Monticello, according to its first plan, was infinitely superior to all other houses in America, in point of taste and convenience; but at that time Mr. Jefferson had studied taste and the fine arts in books only. His travels in Europe have supplied him with models; he has appropriated them to his design; and his new plan, the execution of which is already much advanced, will be accomplished before the end of next year, and then his house will certainly deserve to be ranked with the most pleasant mansions in France and England."

In order to increase the self-sufficiency of the farm during all of these building pursuits, he set up a respectable nailery on the estate; he wrote to Démeunier, a French encyclopedist, in April 1795:

In our private pursuits it is a great advantage that every honest employment is deemed honorable. I am myself a nail-maker. On returning home after an absence of ten years, I found my farms so much deranged that I saw evidently they would be a burden to me instead of a support till I could regenerate them; & consequently that it was necessary for me to find some other resource in the meantime. I thought for awhile of taking up the manufacture of pot-ash, which requires but small advances of money. I concluded at length however to begin a manufacture of nails, which needs little or no capital, & I now employ a dozen little boys from 10. to 16. years of age, overlooking all the details of their business myself & drawing from it a profit on which I can get along till I can put my farms into a course of yielding profit. My new trade of nail-making is to me in this country what an additional title of nobility or the ensigns of a new order are in Europe.

Jefferson liked to deceive himself that he was nothing more than a farmer in retirement. When Madison tried to arouse his dormant ambitions and lively curiosity, Jefferson protested weakly, in the spring of 1795, "The little spice of ambition which I had in my younger days has long since evaporated, and I set still less store by a posthumous than present name." He repeated his determination to Randolph when the president asked for his help in the domestic emergency that arose over the Whisky Rebellion: "No circumstances, my dear Sir, will ever more tempt me to engage in anything public. I thought myself perfectly fixed in this determination when I left Philadelphia, but every day & hour since has added to its inflexibility." But try as hard as he would, and protest as vociferously as he did, it was inevitable that Jefferson could remain for only a limited time divorced and detached from the clamor of the outside world. His friends, particularly Madison and Monroe—good fellow Republicans—kept him informed of the activities of his enemies, the Federalists and Hamiltonians in Philadelphia, skillfully baiting him with hints, stirring him to smoldering rage, and asking for his advice.

Blue Ridge Mountains near Charlottesville.

Early in 1796 Jefferson dropped his pretense that he had no interest in politics. During this election year it became generally known that President Washington would not be a candidate for a third term. The field was wide open. The political atmosphere grew thick with tension as party lines tightened and the names of leading candidates for the high office were discussed and debated. It was certain that the vice president, John Adams, would be a candidate for the presidency and have the support of the Federalists and other conservative interests in general. To the planters of the South, the farmers of the West, and the urban mechanics and artisans of the North, Thomas Jefferson was the logical choice to lead the Republicans and radical-democratic forces. The main problem was persuading him to accept *the candidacy. As early as February, Madison urged him to declare himself a candidate for the presidency: "I intreat you not to procrastinate, much less abandon, your historical task. Your owe it to yourself, to truth, to the world." Jefferson would not budge from his political seclusion: "Politics, a subject I never loved, and now hate," he wrote Adams on February 28, 1796. Madison and Monroe feared that if the Republican party drafted Jefferson as their candidate, he might balk publicly and thereby ruin the party in the election.*

Jefferson's ambiguous attitude and silence were taken for consent, so the Republicans nominated him for the presidency. He accepted the nomination by the simple process of not protesting against it. Politics kept on pursuing him, in spite of himself. He was quite sincere when he declared: "I have no ambition to govern men; no passion which would lead me to delight to ride in a storm." The rawness of politics and the barbs of criticism were a torture to him; nevertheless he could not abstain. He was utterly sincere in his wish to have nothing to do with public affairs, but he was equally sincere in his desire to see his political ideas triumph. Had he definitely and publicly repudiated all claims to the nomination, Aaron Burr, De Witt Clinton, and other lesser lights would have been only too happy to run for the highest office. Therefore, if there was deception in his course, it was nothing more than self-deception.

News of the election came in with maddening slowness, but by the middle of December Jefferson sensed that the election would go against him. He instructed Madison that, in case of a tie, the Republicans should give their vote to Adams. Scrutinizing himself, he found that the unmerited abuse he had been subjected to as governor of Virginia and secretary of state still rankled, and he frankly had no heart for the job of president. Knowing his sensitiveness, many of his friends worried lest he would refuse the vice-presidency; but hearing the rumors, Jefferson wrote a reassuring letter to James Sullivan:

The idea that I would accept the office of President, but not that of Vice President of the U S, had not its origin with me. I never thought of questioning the free exercise of the right of my fellow citizens, to marshal those whom they call into their service according to their fitness, nor ever presumed that they were not the best judges of these. Had I indulged a wish in what manner they should dispose of me, it would precisely have coincided with what they have done. Neither the splendor, nor the power, nor the difficulties, nor the fame or defamation, as may happen, attached to the first magistracy, have any attractions for me.

The result of the election was as Jefferson had anticipated, except the vote had come much nearer an equality than he had expected. When the electoral votes were finally counted in February 1797, it was found that Adams had 71 votes and was declared president, and Jefferson with 68, the next highest, became vice-president. A shift of two votes would have given him the presidency.

On February 20, 1797, Vice-President-elect Jefferson left Monticello for Philadelphia. He was re-entering public life, little suspecting that it would be twelve more years before he could retire again to Monticello to resume his life of an "Antediluvian patriarch" on his farm.

CHAPTER XIII

VICE-PRESIDENT
(1797–1801)

WHEN *Jefferson arrived in Philadelphia to attend the inauguration of the new president on March 4, 1797, he viewed the vice-presidency with a considerable degree of coolness. "The second office of this government is honorable & easy, the first is but a splendid misery," he wrote Elbridge Gerry in May. By contrast, in 1789 its first occupant, Vice-President Adams, had written his wife: "My country has in its wisdom contrived for me the most insignificant office that ever the invention of man contrived or his imagination conceived." Now that Adams had defeated Jefferson for the presidency, both seemed genuinely pleased with the outcome of the election.*

Ten days after taking his oath of office, Jefferson quit his post and returned to Monticello to examine the building in progress and to pursue his agricultural and scientific interests. In a letter to Benjamin Rush he voiced the hope and expectation that he could take his official duties lightly:

I thank you too for your congratulations on the public call on me to undertake the 2d office in the U S, but still more for the justice you do me in viewing as I do the *escape* from the first. I have no wish to meddle again in public affairs, being happier at home than I can be anywhere else. Still less do I wish to engage in an office where it would be impossible to satisfy either friends or foes, and least of all at a moment when the storm is about to burst, which has been conjuring up for four years past. If I am to act however, a more tranquil & unoffending station could not have been found for me, nor one so analogous to the dispositions of my mind. It will give me philosophical evenings in the winter, & rural days in summer.

All too soon he was compelled to leave Monticello. Adams called an extraordinary session of Congress for May 15th, a summons that Jefferson dreaded, for it had an ominous ring. He feared that a declaration of war against France would be the order of the day, for, as he observed, "the President did not need the assistance of Congress to continue in peace."

Jefferson was greatly alarmed over the situation, and desperately hoped that war could be avoided. A Directory of five power-lusting politicians, more interested in national expansion and personal profit than anything else, ruled France. The Directory objected to the maritime measures of the Jay Treaty as not merely unneutral but pro-British, and contemptuously dismissed American neutral rights and played havoc with merchant shipping. Jefferson was optimistic and wrote to Madison:

I do not believe mr. A wishes war with France; nor do I believe he will truckle to England as servilely as has been done. If he assumes this front at once, and shews that he means to attend to self-respect & national dignity with both the nations, perhaps the depredations of both on our commerce may be amicably arrested. I think we should begin first with those who first begin with us, and, by an example on them, acquire a right to re-demand the respect from which the other party has departed.

Adams had, in fact, discreetly sounded a note of reconciliation to the opposition party in his inaugural address. He was pleased with himself and wrote his wife that his oration left "scarcely a dry eye but Washington's" and "all agreed that, taken together, it was the sublimest thing ever exhibited in America." Hamilton condemned the speech, saying it was "temporizing" and "a lure for the favor of his opponents at the expense of his sincerity." Responsible leaders on both sides were anxious to avoid war with either England or France, but the pressure on Adams from Hamilton to make an alliance with England and provoke or declare war on France was at times severe.

Congress opened its session in an inflamed atmosphere, with the question before it, as Jefferson dreaded, one of war or peace. The country was split into bitter pro-French and pro-British factions. It was with a peculiarly helpless feeling of apprehension that Jefferson watched the march of events. As party passion ran high, Adams decided to attempt to find a modus vivendi with the truculent rulers of France by sending a triumvirate of special plenipotentiaries to Paris to negotiate for peace. He finally settled on John Marshall of Virginia, Charles Cotesworth Pinckney of South Carolina, and Elbridge Gerry of Massachusetts. Jefferson wrote a letter of congratulation to Gerry "with infinite joy," urg-

ing him to accept the post and to press for peace.

Peace is undoubtedly at present the first object of our nation. Interest & honor are also national considerations. But interest, duly weighed, is in favor of peace even at the expence of spoliations past & future; & honor cannot now be an object. The insults & injuries committed on us by both the belligerent parties, from the beginning of 1793 to this day, & still continuing, cannot now be wiped off by engaging in war with one of them. As there is great reason to expect this is the last campaign in Europe, it would certainly be better for us to rub thro this year, as we have done through the four preceding ones, and hope that on the restoration of peace, we may be able to establish some plan for our foreign connections more likely to secure our peace, interest & honor, in future. Our countrymen have divided themselves by such strong affections, to the French & the English, that nothing will secure us internally but a divorce from both nations; and this must be the object of every real American, and it's attainment is practicable without much self-denial. But for this, peace is necessary. Be assured of this, my dear Sir, that if we engage in a war during our present passions, & our present weakness in some quarters, that our Union runs the greatest risk of not coming out of that war in the shape in which it enters it.

The passions and hostilities of which Jefferson spoke so earnestly had risen to an unprecedented degree.

With the mission chosen to seek for a peaceable solution of the difficulties with France, Jefferson's worst fears, at least, had not been realized. Congress adjourned and Jefferson left Philadelphia looking forward to the rural

Philosophical Hall, home of the American Philosophical Society, Philadelphia, where Jefferson joined other philosophers and scientists in "promoting useful knowledge."

quiet of Monticello, where he could "exchange the roar & tumult of bulls & bears, for the prattle of my grand-children & senile rest." His eagerness to return was enhanced with the recent news that Maria—his affectionate Polly —had fallen in love with John Wayles Eppes, one of her innumerable cousins, and wanted to be married in the fall. He wrote his other daughter, Martha, with a light heart:

I now see our fireside formed into a groupe, no one member of which has a fibre in their composition which can ever produce any jarring or jealousies among us. No irregular passions, no dangerous bias, which may render problematical the future fortunes and happiness of our descendants.

On October 13, 1797, Jefferson happily saw Maria married to young Eppes. In early December he returned to the scene of strife in Philadelphia, where Congress was already back in session marking time, waiting for news from Paris. In March bad news came. A French decree had been issued making neutral ships carrying enemy goods subject to confiscation. American shipowners and merchants were in consternation, members of Congress—at least the Federalists—were furious, and Jefferson was thunderstruck. Meanwhile dispatches from the American envoys, who had been refused official recognition, had arrived containing incredible news. Tallyrand, the minister of foreign affairs under the Directory, had proposed insulting terms to the Americans through three obscure agents, distinguished by the letters X, Y, and Z, suggesting that a large bribe for his own private pocket and an annual cash tribute to France—repayment indefinite—might lead to favorable terms and facilitate negotiations. The surprised envoys turned down the high-handed offer with indignation.

When the Senate decided to publish the dispatches, the American people, never difficult to stir up, went into a violent war hysteria. "Millions for defense, but not one cent for tribute" became a ringing slogan. Many Republicans joined in the demand for strong measures to vindicate the national honor, and for a moment party lines seemed to be almost obliterated. Jefferson's practiced eye saw the danger at the end of March. "The question of war & peace depends now on a toss of cross & pile," he wrote Madison. "If we could but gain this season, we should be saved."

The administration of John Adams was lifted to a dizzy height of popularity by the momentary passions of an inflamed public opinion. But instead of declaring war, the Federalists were determined to seize the opportunity of stamping out the Republican opposition at home. An epidemic of galloping xenophobia led to repressive legislation with the aim of deporting French propagandists, English infidels, and Irish agitators. In the summer of 1798 the Federalist Congress, against the advice of cooler heads in the party, pushed their advantage hard and passed the Alien and Sedition Acts, designed to choke off agitation and to stifle criticism of the administration and its policies.

The Alien Law authorized the president to order any alien whom he judged dangerous to peace and liberty to depart from the United States, and imposed fines and imprisonment on those who refused to obey the order. The Sedition Law was much more formidable to the opponents of government; it was so broad and inclusive that it virtually abolished the Bill of Rights. It inflicted heavy fines and imprisonment on any who should combine or conspire to oppose government measures, or should utter any false, scandalous, or malicious writing against the government, the Congress, or the president. Most detestable of all, the act attempted to crush all political opposition by making criticism of Federalist officials a crime. The only remedy was to adjourn as soon as possible, for as Jefferson told Madison, "To separate Congress now, will be withdrawing the fire from under a boiling pot." Two days after passing this statute—on July 16, 1798—Congress adjourned.

Jefferson was fighting mad; fearing the consequences, he persisted, nevertheless, in seeing some faint hope. He predicted a "Federalist reign of terror" and coolly waited for its effects as he continued to preside over the Senate with impressive serenity.

For my own part, I consider those laws as merely an experiment on the American mind, to see how far it will bear an avowed violation of the constitution. If this goes down we shall immediately see attempted another act of Congress, declaring that the President shall continue in office during life, reserving to another occasion the transfer of the succession to his heirs, and the establishment of the Senate for life.... That these things are in contemplation, I have no doubt; nor can I be confident of their failure, after the dupery of which our countrymen have shewn themselves susceptible.

All over the country men were being jailed, fined, and persecuted by partisan judges and packed juries because they dared to express their opinions. These were dark days, but thanks to the prudent foresight and matchless fortitude of Jefferson the Republican party survived the ordeal.

Jefferson as vice-president could not openly do very much about the persecutions under the Sedition Act, but as leader of his party he could not refrain from acting. When he went home after the adjournment of Congress he remained silent for two months. Throughout the country a growing host of people looked up to him to raise his voice in protest against these measures, and to supply the leadership against the raging reaction of the zealous Federalists. Jefferson was thinking and acting, but in his own indirect way. Some time in September, working in the strictest secrecy, Jefferson commenced work on a manifesto or series of resolutions—the so-called Kentucky Resolutions—aimed at the centralizing and dictatorial encroachments of Federalism.

For the secrecy there was good and sufficient reason. Jefferson was vice-president of the United States, and these resolutions were an appeal from the authority of the federal government to the authority of the states. They proclaimed boldly the right and duty of the states to declare measures of the national government unconstitutional and void, and hinted even at the last resort of secession from that government—"that these and successive acts of the same character, unless arrested at the threshold, will necessarily drive these States into revolution and blood."

The resolutions, as Jefferson shaped them into final form, expounded a theory of federal compact which made the several states the final arbiters of Constitutional construction and the sole guardian of their own absolute powers against the delegated powers of the national government. Madison, meanwhile, had drafted the Virginia Resolutions, which, even with Jefferson's revisions, were more general and moderate than Jefferson's. The Kentucky Resolutions were adopted with virtual unanimity by the Kentucky legislature in early November 1798; the Virginia Resolutions overwhelmingly carried in the legislature in late December. The first heavy gauge shots had been fired in the war on the Federalists.

In late December 1798 Jefferson returned to Philadelphia to attend the opening of the third session of the Fifth Congress, where he continued to preside over the Senate with scrupulous impartiality and impressive serenity. The crisis was over and the war fever rapidly subsided. Jefferson gave no credit to Adams, but to the American people.

The spirit of 1776 is not dead. It has only been slumbering. The body of the American people is substantially republican. But their virtuous feelings have been played on by some fact with more fiction; they have been the dupes of artful manœuvres, & made for a moment to be willing instruments in forging chains for themselves. But time & truth have dissipated the delusion, & opened their eyes.

In the darkest days of Federalist reaction, Jefferson's function was to inspire, to motivate, to stimulate, to clarify. He wanted his friends and followers to understand the fundamental issues and to act upon them in the light of reason. He placed all his faith in the education of the public. He wrote long letters on a wide variety of subjects so that men would not fall victim to flimsy arguments and false appeals. One of his letters written to his vacillating friend, Elbridge Gerry, in January 1799 was a declaration of the principles he did not fear to espouse. It is a fine example of epistolary campaign literature; it explains his objectives and states his basic beliefs—the most luminous exposition of the Jeffersonian doctrine ever made.

I do then, with sincere zeal, wish an inviolable preservation of our present federal constitution, according to the true sense in which it was adopted by the States, that in which it was advocated by it's friends, & not that which it's enemies apprehended, who therefore became it's enemies; and I am opposed to the monarchising it's features by the forms of it's administration, with a view to conciliate a first transition to a President & Senate for life, & from that to a hereditary tenure of these offices, & thus to worm out the elective principle. I am for preserving to the States the powers not yielded by them to the Union, & to the legislature of the Union it's constitutional share in the division of powers; and I am not for transferring all the powers of the States to the general government, & all those of that

government to the Executive branch. I am for a government rigorously frugal & simple, applying all the possible savings of the public revenue to the discharge of the national debt; and not for a multiplication of officers & salaries merely to make partisans, & for increasing, by every device, the public debt, on the principle of it's being a public blessing. I am for relying, for internal defence, on our militia solely, till actual invasion, and for such a naval force only as may protect our coasts and harbors from such depredations as we have experienced; and not for a standing army in time of peace, which may overawe the public sentiment; nor for a navy, which, by it's own expenses and the eternal wars in which it will implicate us, will grind us with public burthens, & sink us under them. I am for free commerce with all nations; political connection with none; & little or no diplomatic establishment. And I am not for linking ourselves by new treaties with the quarrels of Europe; entering that field of slaughter to preserve their balance, or joining in the confederacy of kings to war against the principles of liberty. I am for freedom of religion, & against all maneuvres to bring about a legal ascendancy of one sect over another: for freedom of the press, & against all violations of the constitution to silence by force & not by reason the complaints or criticisms, just or unjust, of our citizens against the conduct of their agents. And I am for encouraging the progress of science in all it's branches; and not for raising a hue and cry against the sacred name of philosophy; for awing the human mind by stories of raw-head & bloody bones to a distrust of its own vision, & to repose implicitly on that of others; to go backwards instead of forwards to look for improvement; to believe that government, religion, morality, & every other science were in the highest perfection in ages of the darkest ignorance, and that nothing can ever be devised more perfect than what was established by our forefathers. To these I will add, that I was a sincere well-wisher to the success of the French revolution, and still wish it may end in the establishment of a free & well-ordered republic; but I have not been insensible under the atrocious depredations they have committed on our commerce.

He concluded this platform for the Republican Party with a moving declaration of pure and disinterested patriotism:

The first object of my heart is my own country. In that is embarked my family, my fortune, & my own existence. I have not one farthing of interest, nor one fibre of attachment out of it, nor a single motive of preference of any one nation to another, but in proportion as they are more or less friendly to us.

This remarkable letter, written in the midst of unprecedented political strife and street riots in Philadelphia, transcended the circumstances of the moment. After nearly thirty years of political life, Jefferson had defined his own political creed and drafted the first program for his party.

For sheer virulence and bitterness, the campaign of 1800 was unlike anything ever experienced in America before. Each side knew what was at stake, and the strategy on both sides was aimed at the glittering prize. As the election year got underway, Jefferson remained at Monticello and calmly continued with his routine and attended to his private affairs, busy with his nail factory and brick kiln. He neither orated nor campaigned. But as the campaign storm broke, he was made the target of monstrous abuse and defamation. The Federalists portrayed him as a thief, a coward, a

libertine, an infidel, and an atheist. *The attacks on his religion did not budge him from his determination to ignore them. He had too great a contempt for his detractors to dignify them with a reply.*

I know that I might have filled the courts of the United States with actions for these slanders, and have ruined perhaps many persons who are not innocent. But this would be no equivalent to the loss of character. I leave them, therefore, to the reproof of their own consciences. If these do not condemn them, there will yet come a day when the false witness will meet a judge who has not slept over his slanders.

But from his friends Jefferson could not conceal his anger at the violent attacks by the clergy on his religious views. At the height of the campaign of vilification, he gave voice to one of his angriest yet most enduring statements on the religious issue—freedom versus intolerance—in a letter to Dr. Benjamin Rush:

I promised you a letter on Christianity, which I have not forgotten. On the contrary, it is because I have reflected on it, that I find much more time necessary for it than I can at present dispose of. I have a view of the subject which ought to displease neither the rational Christian nor Deists, and would reconcile many to a character they have too hastily rejected. I do not know that it would reconcile the *genus irritabile vatum* who are all in arms against me. Their hostility is on too interesting ground to be softened. The delusion into which the X. Y. Z. plot shewed it possible to push the people; the successful experiment made under the prevalence of that delusion on the clause of the constitution, which, while it secured the freedom of the press, covered also the freedom of religion, had given to the clergy a very favorite hope of obtaining an establishment of a particular form of Christianity thro' the U. S.; and as every sect believes its own form the true one, every one perhaps hoped for his own, but especially the Episcopalians & Congregationalists. The returning good sense of our country threatens abortion to their hopes, & they believe that any portion of power confided to me, will be exerted in opposition to their schemes. And they believe rightly; for I have sworn upon the altar of god, eternal hostility against every form of tyranny over the mind of man.

Jefferson remained at Monticello until the end of November 1800, out of the heat of the conflict. He arrived at the city of Washington —the new capital of the United States since June—to assume his final duties as vice-president and to await the election returns, which came in slowly. When the electoral vote was finally counted, it was found that though Adams was defeated, Jefferson was not elected. This paradoxical situation resulted from a confused electoral law, which did not stipulate that the electors should specify which of the candidates was to be president and which vice-president. Each elector voted for two candidates, and the one with the highest number of votes was declared president. Adams and Thomas Pinckney were defeated with 65 and 64 electoral votes respectively, but the Republican vote stood at 73 votes for Jefferson and his running mate, Aaron Burr. The Jeffersonians had a majority of the total votes cast, but they had no president. The election, therefore, had to be thrown into the House of Representatives, which, under the Constitution, had the power to break the tie. A bitter deadlock ensued in the House of Representatives as ballots were taken numerous times each day between February 12 and 17, 1801, before Jefferson was finally elected.

The inauguration ceremonies were simple but dignified. John Marshall, chief justice of the Supreme Court, was asked by Jefferson himself to administer the oath, and on March 4, 1801, the third president of the United States was inaugurated.

CHAPTER XIV

TRIUMPHANT REPUBLICANISM (1801–1805)

Before the bitterness of the turbulent election campaign had subsided, Americans realized that with the election of Jefferson the first era of American national politics had ended and that a new and different one was about to begin. Jefferson's accession to the presidency was, naturally, viewed with sharply diverse feelings. The more bitter Federalists foresaw the end of the world, the subversion of orderly government, and the trampling of property-less mobs through the streets of cities; while their even more embittered adherents among the New England clergy prophesied the reign of antichrist and the death of all religion. The Republicans, however, intoxicated with the wine of victory, hailed the dawn of a new and more glorious era, in which the will of the people would prevail. It was a victory for democracy in their view, when free men by open elections had chosen a leader who believed in equality for all men, in opportunity for all men, in toleration for all men, and above all in government by all men.

Jefferson was conscious of a double responsibility: to the American people and to the rest of the world. He sincerely believed that the successful functioning of American democracy should serve as a model for the rest of mankind:

A just and solid republican government maintained here, will be a standing monument & example for the aim & imitation of the people of other countries; and I join with you in the hope and belief that they will see, from our example, that a free government is of all others the most energetic; that the inquiry which has been excited among the mass of mankind by our revolution & it's consequences, will ameliorate the condition of man over a great portion of the globe.

The battle over, Jefferson's primary desire was to bring about a reunion of former political opponents. The policy of the new administration would not be one of reprisals. His inaugural address was an eloquent appeal for national unity and conciliation:

Called upon to undertake the duties of the first Executive office of our country, I . . . declare a sincere consciousness that the task is above my talents, & that I approach it with those anxious & awful presentiments, which the greatness of the charge, & the weakness of my powers so justly inspire. . . .

All too will bear in mind this sacred principle that though the will of the Majority is in all cases to prevail, that will, to be rightful,

must be reasonable: that the Minority possess their equal rights, which equal laws must protect, & to violate would be oppression.

Let us then, fellow citizens, unite with one heart & one mind; let us restore to social intercourse that harmony & affection, without which Liberty, & even Life itself, are but dreary things.

And let us reflect that having banished from our land that religious intolerance under which mankind so long bled & suffered we have yet gained little, if we countenance a political intolerance, as despotic, as wicked & capable of as bitter & bloody persecution. . . .

But every difference of opinion, is not a difference of principle. We have called, by different names, brethren of the same principle. We are all republicans: we are all federalists.

Jefferson's immediate and most pressing problem was what to do about the matter of removals from and appointments to office. Jefferson's attitude on this question was, throughout, one of firmness and consistency. When his election by the House of Representatives hung in the balance, he had refused to bind himself to retain Federalist officeholders in their positions. Now that he had won, he refused as stoutly the importunities of Republicans who clamored for the dismissal of their opponents. About the Federalist judges he could do nothing; but he could sweep out Federalist district attorneys, marshals, justices of the peace, and customs collectors. Removing people from office, however, was an ordeal he did not find congenial. In theory Jefferson had no intention of punishing men for their opinions:

My principles, and those always received by the republicans, do not admit removing any person from office merely for a difference of political opinion. Malversations in office, & the exerting of official influence to control the freedom of election are good causes for removal.

But the Republican clamor for political fleshpots rose to overwhelming proportions: "My position is painful enough between federalists who cry out on the first touch of their monopoly, and republicans who clamor for universal removal," he wrote in the summer of 1801. Jefferson was well aware of the practicability of a strong political machine and of the power of the "spoils system" as the Constitution permitted the president to use it. "A person who wishes to make [patronage] an engine of self-elevation may do wonders with it," he wrote James Sullivan in 1808. All this wretched business in position-peddling and office-mongering was distasteful to him, and he consequently made few removals. In 1799, before he had practical experience of the fact, he remarked to Tench Coxe that "whenever a man has cast a longing eye on [offices], a rottenness begins in his conduct." Now he found that

The task of appointment is a heavy one indeed. He on whom it falls may envy the lot of Sisyphus or Ixion. Their agonies were of the body; this of the mind. Yet, like the office of hangman, it must be executed by some one. It has been assigned to me and made my duty. I make up my mind to it therefore, and abandon all regard to consequences.

By the end of Jefferson's first administration a total of about one-third of the officials appointed by Adams were removed. In their place Jefferson appointed those men who were friendly to his ideals and on whose loyalty he could rely.

In spite of these difficulties, the new admin-

The President's House, later the White House, designed by James Hoban; work was begun on the building in July 1792.

Romantic classicism: the President's House in Washington, where Jefferson lived from 1801 to 1809.

Roman classicism: the Temple of Diana at Nîmes, which Jefferson visited in 1787.

istration went ahead with an impressive program of political reforms. Jefferson and his secretary of the treasury attacked the problem of economy on three fronts: there was to be no more borrowing; the national debt was to be extinguished by systematic payments of principal and interest; and expenditures were to be drastically reduced. In his first annual message of December 8, 1801, he explained his theory of the functions and obligations of the federal government to substitute economy for taxation:

When we consider that this government is charged with the external and mutual relations only of these states; that the states themselves have principal care of our persons, our property, and our reputation, constituting the great field of human concerns, we may well doubt whether our organization is not too complicated, too expensive; whether offices or officers have not been multiplied unnecessarily, and sometimes injuriously to the service they

were meant to promote. . . . Considering the general tendency to multiply offices and dependencies, and to increase expense to the ultimate term of burden which the citizen can bear, it behooves us to avail ourselves of every occasion which presents itself for taking off the surcharge; that it may never be seen here that, after leaving to labor the smallest portion of its earnings on which it can subsist, government shall itself consume the residue of what it was instituted to guard.

Next he recommended the specific provisions for reducing the expenditures. The army establishment was entirely too large: "For defence against invasion, their number is as nothing; nor is it conceived needful or safe that a standing army should be kept up in time of peace for that purpose." As for the navy, "A small force will probably continue to be wanted in the Mediterranean," but he added that work on certain navy yards be "suspended or slackened." Jefferson's party stood for a

The Capitol, Washington, D. C.

strong tariff, while the Federalist advocated internal taxes. Among the direct taxes Jefferson abolished was the excise on distilled liquors. At the end of his first term, Jefferson was able to proclaim that "it may be the pleasure and pride of an American to ask what farmer, what mechanic, what labourer, ever sees a tax-gatherer of the United States?"

One of the most striking episodes of reform of Jefferson's administration was his assault on the federal judiciary. He was driven to this conflict by the dynamics of his ideas as well as by the logic of his position. Adams had packed judicial posts with his own appointees of bitter-end Federalists. In his first message to Congress in December 1801, Jefferson gave an indication of his intentions to put a bridle on the judiciary: "The judiciary system of the United States, and especially that portion of it recently erected, will of course present itself to the contemplation of Congress." He offered evidence that there was not enough business to warrant the number of judges. In battling the judiciary, Jefferson followed a definite constitutional theory: the framers of the Constitution had intended the three branches of the government to check—not to dominate—each other. He expressed this idea clearly in a letter to Abigail Adams, where he explained why he granted pardons to the victims of the Sedition Act:

The judges, believing the law constitutional, had a right to pass a sentence of fine and imprisonment, because that power was placed in their hands by the constitution. But the Executive, believing the law to be unconstitutional, was bound to remit the execution of it; because that power has been confided to him by the constitution. That instrument meant that it's co-ordinate branches should be checks on each other. But the opinion which gives to the judges the right to decide what laws are constitutional, and what not, not only for themselves in their own sphere of action, but for the legislature and executive also in their spheres, would make the judiciary a despotic branch.

The first countermeasure of the Republicans had been to repeal the hateful Judiciary Act of the preceding session, by which the scope of the federal courts had been extended. But while Jefferson was waiting for the proper moment to solve the problem of the judiciary, Chief Justice John Marshall rendered a decision in Marbury v. Madison, *which rebuked Jefferson directly and asserted the supremacy of the Supreme Court. The dangerous implications of Marshall's decision were not lost on Jefferson, who sensed immediately that this was a threat to free government in the future. He struck back at the judges, and tried to impeach Justice Samuel Chase of the Supreme Court, an intemperate reactionary of exceptional virulence who reveled in outraging public opinion. When the Senate refused to impeach Chase, Jefferson failed in his attempt to put a permanent curb on the judiciary. But the threat of impeachment had its effect and momentarily silenced the judiciary.*

However, the hostile Federalist press was far from silent and took advantage of Jefferson's belief in the freedom of the press. No matter how greatly newspapers abused their freedom, it was vital, Jefferson felt, for democracy that freedom not be checked. The Federalists "fill their newspapers with falsehoods, calumnies, and audacities," he wrote to a friend, but "I shall protect them in the right of lying and calumniating." In 1804 he wrote to Mazzei, "Every word of mine which they can get hold of, however innocent, however orthodox, is twisted, tormented, perverted, and like the words of holy writ, are made to mean everything but what they were intended to mean." To Thomas Cooper he remarked wryly, "You know that if I write as a text that two and two are four, it serves to make volumes of sermons of slander and abuse." Nevertheless, he was determined that nothing should block the "experiment" in freedom; he wrote John Tyler:

No experiment can be more interesting than that we are now trying, which we trust will end in establishing the fact that man may be governed by reason & truth. Our first object should therefore be to leave open to him all the avenues to truth. The most effectual hitherto found is the freedom of the press. It is therefore the first shut up by those who fear the investigation of their actions.

After Jefferson's death, Madison observed with insight that "no man more than Mr. Jefferson, regarded the freedom of the press as an essential safeguard to free Government."

Another reform Jefferson initiated and guided through Congress early in his first administration was an amendment of the Naturalization Law—passed during the hysteria over aliens—which shortened the term of residence for naturalization from fourteen to five years.

I cannot omit recommending a revisal of the laws on the subject of naturalization. Considering the ordinary chances of human life, a denial of citizenship under a residence of fourteen years is a denial to a great proportion of those who ask it, and controls a policy pursued from their first settlement by many of these States, and still believed of consequence to their prosperity. And shall we refuse the unhappy fugitives from distress that hospitality which the savages of the wilderness extended

The Second Bank of the United States, Philadelphia.

to our fathers arriving in this land? Shall oppressed humanity find no asylum on this globe?

Finally, Jefferson's first term commanded the respect and praise even of the unreconciled. In 1828, after years spent in vitriolic hatred of Jefferson, John Randolph of Roanoke said in a public speech: "I have never seen but one Administration which seriously and in good faith was disposed to give up its patronage, and was willing to go farther than Congress, or even the people themselves, so far as Congress represents their feelings, desired; and that was the first Administration of Thomas Jefferson. He, sir, was the only man I knew or ever heard of, who really, truly, and honestly, not only said Nolo episcopari, *but actually refused the mitre."*

Oak Hill, Loudoun County, Virginia; James Monroe's house, from designs
by James Hoban incorporating suggestions by Jefferson.

CHAPTER XV

PROTECTIVE IMPERIALISM AND TERRITORIAL EXPANSION (1801–1805)

Uᴺᴛɪʟ *the spring of 1802, the attention of President Jefferson and the country was devoted almost exclusively to domestic problems. But soon events beyond his control rudely shattered the president's dream of political isolation from European entanglements and the rest of the world. News reached this country that the weak and decadent Spanish government by the secret Treaty of San Ildefonso in October 1800 had ceded the vast Louisiana Territory and Florida back to an aggressive and powerful France.*

When the peace-loving Jefferson learned of the retrocession, he immediately realized the importance and threatening implications of having an ardent and ambitious neighbor like Napoleon Bonaparte in control of New Orleans and in a position to affect the destiny of every American living west of the Allegheny Mountains. Although it was inconvenient to have Spain astride the mouth of the Mississippi, that country was too weak to be dangerous to the United States. France, by contrast, was strong and restless and could threaten American control of the vast interior of the Mississippi Valley. With painful clarity Jefferson

saw that as long as a strong foreign power held New Orleans, the United States would be drawn into European politics. This country would face the choice of either submitting to dictation and a permanent status of inferiority, or fighting for control of the Mississippi and the entire West. This was elementary politics dictated by the stubborn facts of geography.

The destruction of the president's isolationist fences roused him to vigilance and immediate activity. Jefferson wrote a lengthy confidential letter to Robert R. Livingston, the American minister in France, that is remarkable for its revelation of his realpolitik. Although some extremists were calling for immediate war, and even though Jefferson himself was greatly disturbed by the Louisiana situation, he preferred to try negotiation first. His analyses of courses to be pursued and possible concessions and alternative compromises to be chosen were composed and deliberate.

There is on the globe one single spot, the possessor of which is our natural and habitual enemy. It is New Orleans, through which the produce of three-eighths of our territory must pass to market, and from its fertility it will ere long yield more than half of our whole produce and contain more than half our inhabitants. France placing herself in that door assumes to us the attitude of defiance. Spain might have retained it quietly for years. Her pacific dispositions, her feeble state, would induce her to increase our facilities there, so that her possession of the place would be hardly felt by us, and it would not perhaps be very long before some circumstance might arise which might make the cession of it to us the price of something of more worth to her. Not so can it ever be in the hands of France. . . . The day that France takes possession of N. Orleans fixes the sentence which is to restrain her forever within her low water mark. It seals the union of two nations who in conjunction can maintain exclusive possession of the ocean. From that moment we must marry ourselves to the British fleet and nation. We must turn all our attentions to a maritime force, for which our resources place us on very high grounds: and having formed and cemented together a power which may render reinforcement of her settlements here impossible to France, make the first cannon, which shall be fired in Europe the signal for tearing up any settlement she may have made, and for holding the two continents of America in sequestration for the common purposes of the united British and American nations. This is not a state of things we seek or desire. It is one which this measure, if adopted by France, forces on us.

This was a remarkable letter, in which his phrasing was deliberately blunt and unequivocal: here Jefferson first enunciated the doctrine—later to be made famous by Monroe—that the American continents were free and independent and not subject to future colonization by European powers. The Anglophobe president, furthermore, warned that he was ready to ally with Britain to keep the French out of New Orleans.

In his famous inaugural address, dealing largely with domestic policies, Jefferson had touched on foreign problems and inserted a clear definition of his attitude towards Europe. He regarded the United States as an experience of vital importance to the whole world, free from the vestigial heritages of feudalism and the anachronistic institutions of the Old World. Man was free as he ought to be as a result of the natural conditions in this isolated setting: "Kindly separated by nature, & a wide ocean, from the exterminating havoc of one quarter of the globe, Too high-minded to endure the degradations of others; Possessing a chosen country, with room enough for all descendants to the 100th & 1,000th generation." This doctrine contained a new and interesting affirmation of unquestionable superiority of the American people over all the peoples of the earth, not only morally but intellectually; Jefferson was beginning to draw, it must be confessed, dangerous conclusions from the uniqueness of America's position.

By the end of the summer of 1802, it appeared that France had every intention of taking possession of Louisiana before entering into any consideration of American offers. Livingston, isolated from his home government by many weeks of tedious communication, groped rather blindly for a solution. He knew that such a step on the part of the French would cause an irresistible outburst of public opinion in America. The situation at home had changed in the interim for the worse. The Spanish authorities in New Orleans suspended in the autumn of 1802 the right of deposit from American merchants. This meant a loss of a million dollars' worth of produce annually by inhabitants of the western territory, and stunt-

Harpers Ferry, at the confluence of the Shenandoah and the Potomac rivers. Jefferson loved the splendid scenery and wild primitive beauty of the mountains and rivers here.

Poplar Forest, Bedford County, near Lynchburg, Virginia. Designed by Jefferson on the basis of the octagon with porticoes in front and rear, the house was frequently used by him in retirement as a country seat.

ing the growth of the West by choking its outlet. Throughout the country there was an outburst of indignation; Jefferson wrote Du Pont de Nemours: "The suspension of the right of deposit at New Orleans, ceded to us by our treaty with Spain, threw our whole country into such a ferment as imminently threatened its peace." The president was furious, but was able to maintain an impressive façade of imperturbability: he knew what he was about, and was determined to either buy New Orleans or fight for it. But when the bad news arrived from Livingston and Du Pont, Jefferson's patience was exhausted and he was goaded into an outburst:

We stand, compleately corrected of the error, that either the government or the nation of France has any remains of friendship for us. The portion of that country which forms an exception, though respectable in weight, is weak in numbers. On the contrary, it appears evident, that an unfriendly spirit prevails in the most important individuals of the government, towards us. In this state of things, we shall so take our distance between the two rival nations, as, remaining disengaged till necessity compels us, we may haul finally to the enemy of that which shall make it necessary. We see all the disadvantageous consequences of taking a side, and shall be forced into it only by a more disagreeable alternative.

There was a direct threat of war; the president himself had lost patience and, apparently, having given up any hope of reaching an agreement, was yielding to the war party of the West.

In January 1803 the Federalists took advantage of the western Republican clamor for free navigation of the Mississippi River by proposing a fiery resolution demanding that

all the documents relating to Louisiana be submitted to them. This serious move to expose Jefferson's delicate negotiations to public gaze and criticism would have unquestionably badly damaged, if not permanently destroyed, whatever chances remained of successfully acquiring the western territory. The administration forces rallied to table the resolution, and met the Federalist assault with a resolution to deliver into the president's hands two million dollars "to defray any expences which may be incurred in relations to the intercourse between the United States and foreign nations" without any strings attached. This was an essential part of a preconceived strategy which Jefferson had worked out with a few Republican leaders in Congress. Something dramatic, he realized, had to be done; he decided to send Monroe on an extraordinary mission to France to work with Livingston in negotiating a final settlement of the Mississippi question. Early in January he wrote Madison and explained that this bold move was necessary because of "the fever into which the western mind is thrown by the affair at N. Orleans stimulated by the mercantile, and generally the federal interest threatens to overbear our peace." The Senate approved Monroe's nomination without much debate and Jefferson immediately urged him to accept.

You possess the unlimited confidence of the administration and of the western people; and generally of the republicans everywhere; and were you to refuse to go, no other man can be found who does this. The measure has already silenced the Feds. here. Congress will no longer be agitated by them: and the country will become calm as fast as the information extends over it. All eyes, all hopes, are now fixed on you; and were you to decline, the chagrin would be universal, and would shake under your feet the high ground on which you stand with the public. Indeed I know nothing which would produce such a shock, for on the event of this mission depends the future destinies of this republic.

But the philosophic president was peering into the future and had a vision of a greater America, one extending even beyond the limits of the Louisiana Purchase. Could a self-imposed border continue to hold for generations to come against the irresistible pressures of a fast-growing population seeking new lands? He looked to the natural boundary of the far-distant Pacific Ocean. In January 1803, a week before Monroe's appointment as a special envoy to Paris, Jefferson sent a confidential message to Congress containing a proposal to appoint an expedition to explore the territory west of the Mississippi under the guise of "a literary pursuit."

An intelligent officer, with ten or twelve chosen men, fit for the enterprise, and willing to undertake it, taken from our posts, where they may be spared without inconvenience, might explore the whole line, even to the Western Ocean, have conferences with the natives on the subject of commercial intercourse, get admission among them for our traders, as others are admitted, agree on convenient deposits for an interchange of articles, and return with the information acquired, in the course of two summers. . . . While other civilized nations have encountered great expense to enlarge the boundaries of knowledge by undertaking voyages of discovery, and for other literary purposes, in various parts and directions, our nation seems to owe to the same object, as well as to its own interests, to explore this, the only line of easy communication across the continent, and so directly traversing

our own part of it. The interests of commerce place the principal object within the constitutional powers and care of Congress, and that it should incidentally advance the geographical knowledge of our own continent, cannot be but an additional gratification.

Congress agreed, and Jefferson made the expedition his own concern. He chose as the "intelligent officer" Meriwether Lewis, his private secretary, who in turn picked as his colleague William Clark of Albemarle, who had been in the army and had seen Indian fighting. The great expedition of exploration under Lewis and Clark soon got under way. These dreams of expansion into the vast new West fired Jefferson's enthusiasm; he drafted detailed instructions to Lewis, raised the funds, and followed the success of the expedition with mounting excitement. From St. Louis the small band of pioneers traveled up the Missouri River into the uncharted wilderness; they finally succeeded in reaching the mouth of the Columbia River before returning to St. Louis, taking two years and four months to make the journey. In his message to Congress in December 1806, Jefferson spoke feelingly of the accomplishments of the Lewis and Clark expedition:

The expedition of Messrs. Lewis and Clarke, for exploring the river Missouri, and the best communication from that to the Pacific ocean, has had all the success which could have been expected. They have traced the Missouri nearly to its source, descended the Columbia to the Pacific ocean, ascertained with accuracy the geography of that interesting communication across our continent, learned the character of the country, of its commerce, and inhabitants; and it is but justice to say that Messrs. Lewis and Clarke, and their brave companions, have by this arduous service deserved well of their country. . . .

These important surveys, in addition to those before possessed, furnished materials for commencing an accurate map of the Mississippi, and its western waters.

The action of Spain in suspending the rights of deposit at New Orleans and closing the river to navigation had rendered imperative an immediate settlement. To Du Pont, who was on an unofficial mission for him, he spoke the language of war:

Our circumstances are so imperious as to admit of no delay as to our course; and the use of the Mississippi so indispensable, that we cannot hesitate one moment to hazard our existence for its maintenance. If we fail in this effort to put it beyond the reach of accident, we see the destinies we have to run, and prepare at once for them.

But at the same time, the government was slowly scaling down its aims to exceedingly modest levels and weakening instructions to its plenipotentiaries, because of the urgency of the situation and the bleak prospects for any sort of settlement. The United States was ready to take even a part of New Orleans and to omit the Floridas altogether, provided it received the rights of deposit and free navigation of the rivers emptying into the Gulf of Mexico. "Peace is our passion, and wrongs might drive us from it," Jefferson told the British. "We prefer trying every other just principle, right and safety, before we recur to war."

For months America waited in anxious suspense to hear something from their negotiators, not knowing that matters were moving swiftly to a surprising denouement. Then

Fireplace at Oak Hill, gift from Marquis de Lafayette to President Monroe.

came the glorious news from Paris! In April 1803, Napoleon, with his plans for an American empire having all gone astray when the French army in Santo Domingo was annihilated by rebellious blacks, and with the long contemplated war with England imminent, decided to sell all of Louisiana to the United States for $15,000,000 in American money. The news of the Great Purchase was divulged at the end of June and hit the country like a summer thunderbolt. Nothing was heard but praise from jubilant Americans who acclaimed "The Immortal Jefferson" who had brought about such magnificent results. In one bold stroke, and with superlative luck, Jefferson had doubled the territory of the country, not by war but through purchase.

Public confidence in Jefferson was immense, and before Congress adjourned in the spring of 1804, the Republican caucus unanimously renominated Jefferson for president. "Never," said John Randolph years later, "was there an administration more brilliant than that of Mr. Jefferson up to this period." But Jefferson's enjoyment of political and personal success was abruptly shattered by personal tragedy. His beautiful daughter Mary Jefferson Eppes, a brilliant and gifted young lady, died at Monticello at the age of twenty-five on April 17, 1804. Jefferson, who was now sixty-one and with only one surviving child, was shaken by this merciless blow as he had not been since his wife's death. To John Page, his boyhood friend who was now governor of Virginia, he poured out his grief with unaccustomed lack of restraint:

Others may lose of their abundance, but I, of my want, have lost even the half of all I had. My evening prospects now hang on the slender thread of a single life. Perhaps I may be destined to see even this last cord of parental affection broken! The hope with which I had looked forward to the moment when, resigning public cares to younger hands, I was to retire to that domestic comfort from which the last great step is to be taken, is fearfully blighted.

But no letter of condolence he received touched him more in his depressed state of mind than one from "her, who once took pleasure in subscribing Herself your Friend, Abigail Adams." It was written in secrecy, without the knowledge of her husband, after a silence of nearly three and a half years filled with bitterness over the political battles of 1800 and 1801. The sensitive wounds were still unhealed, but the stern old woman could not resist a plaintive cry from the heart: "Had you been no other than the private inhabitant of Monticello, I should e'er this time have addrest you, with that sympathy, which a re-

cent event has awakend in my Bosom. But reasons of various kinds withheld my pen, untill the powerfull feelings of my heart, have burst through the restraint, and called upon me to shed the tear of sorrow over the departed remains, of your beloved and deserving daughter, an event which I most sincerely mourn.

"The attachment which I formed for her, when you committed her to my care: upon her arrival in a foreign Land: has remained with me to this hour, and the recent account of her death, which I read in a late paper, brought fresh to my remembrance the strong sensibility she discoverd, tho but a child of nine years of age at having been seperated from her Friends, and country, and brought, as she expressed it, 'to a strange land amongst strangers.' The tender scene of her seperation from me, rose to my recollection, when she clung around my neck and wet my Bosom with her tears, saying 'O! now I have learnt to Love you, why will they tear me from you'

"It has been some time since that I conceived of any event in this Life, which could call forth, feelings of mutual sympathy. But I know how closely entwined around a parents heart, are those chords which bind the filial to the parental Bosom, and when snaped assunder, how agonizing the pangs of seperation."

Jefferson replied in a most affectionate strain, and a short correspondence of seven letters ensued in which the causes of the alienation between Adams and Jefferson were reviewed. But the indomitable old lady was still unsatisfied, and with a tartness all her own, she ended flatly: "I will not Sir any further intrude upon your time, but close this correspondence." Jefferson regretted this prolonged misunderstanding with Mrs. Adams, but six years later these letters would be the basis of a reconciliation between the two aging Argonauts of the Revolutionary struggle.

CHAPTER XVI

THE DIFFICULTIES
OF NEUTRALITY
(1805-1809)

ON *March 4, 1805, Jefferson delivered his second inaugural address and began another term of office in an aura of triumph and universal good feeling. Nothing was permitted to interfere with the harmony of the occasion. Abroad, he declared, "we have endeavored to cultivate the friendship of all nations"; and here at home, "the suppression of unnecessary offices, of useless establishments and expenses, enabled us to discontinue our internal taxes." He turned next to the topic of the purchase of Louisiana—perhaps the most brilliant success of his administration. Some feared its acquisition and thought such an undue extension of our territory would endanger the Union. "But who can limit the extent to which the federative principle may operate effectively?" inquired the ardent expansionist. "The larger our association, the less will it be shaken by local passions; and in any view, is it not better that the opposite bank of the Mississippi should be settled by our own brethren and children, than by strangers of another family?"*

But trouble with Spain over the vaguely defined boundaries of Louisiana and the renewal of war between the European powers in 1803 were beginning to revive grave threats to America's neutral and national rights. It is not without significance that Jefferson concluded his address with a prayer for peace—one he undoubtedly repeated during the four years of his troubled second administration.

I shall now enter on the duties to which my fellow citizens have again called me, and shall proceed in the spirit of those principles which they have approved. I fear not that any motives of interest may lead me astray; I am sensible of no passion which could seduce me knowingly from the path of justice; but the weakness of human nature, and the limits of my own understanding, will produce errors of judgment sometimes injurious to your interests. I shall need, therefore, all the indulgence I have heretofore experienced—the want of it will certainly not lessen with increasing years. I shall need, too, the favor of that Being in whose hands we are, who led our forefathers, as Israel of old, from their native land, and planted them in a country flowing with all the necessaries and comforts of life; who has covered our infancy with his providence, and our riper years with his wisdom and power; and to whose goodness I ask you to join with me in supplications, that he will so enlighten the minds of your servants, guide their councils, and prosper their measures, that whatsoever they do, shall result in your good, and shall secure to you the peace, friendship, and approbation of all nations.

One of Jefferson's domestic troubles that ran like a scarlet thread through the years 1806 and 1807 and exacerbated his personal emotions was the bitter Aaron Burr conspiracy. After Burr left the vice-presidency, discredited as a man and ruined as a politician, he approached Jefferson's enemies with intrigues and machinations aimed toward building for himself a western empire. The mysterious Burr plot against the unity and welfare of the United States was more of an annoyance than a genuine threat to Jefferson; yet, the president was intent on crushing this betrayal. He wrote to Charles Clay:

Burr's enterprise is the most extraordinary since the days of Don Quixot. It is so extravagant that those who know his understanding would not believe it if the proofs admitted doubt. He has meant to place himself on the throne of Montezuma, and extend his empire to the Allegany seizing on N Orleans as the instrument of compulsion for our Western States. I think his undertaking effectually crippled by the activity of Ohio. Whether Kentucky will give him the coup de grace is doubtful; but if he is able to descend the river with any means we are sufficiently prepared at New Orleans.

After Burr was seized and brought to Richmond for trial on a charge of treason, public excitement in the country mounted and Jefferson was busily engaged in checking over-enthusiastic friends, who magnified the proportions of Burr's schemes, and silencing Federalist opponents, who showed marked friendliness to the former vice-president. But what

shocked the president into violent reaction was the strained reasoning and underhand tactics of Chief Justice John Marshall, a diehard Federalist and his bitter personal adversary, who acquitted Burr because the chief justice's calculated definition of treason was such that it could not apply to the defendant. The case amounted to an attack, by Federalist influences, upon the power of the executive to punish treason.

The fact is that the Federalists make Burr's cause their own, and exert their whole influence to shield him from punishment, as they did the adherents of Miranda. And it is unfortunate that federalism is still predominant in our judiciary department, which is consequently in opposition to the legislative & Executive branches, & is able to baffle their measures often.

Although Burr was acquitted by Marshall, the popular contempt for him was so widespread that he was almost lynched and, finally, had to flee the country. Jefferson wrote Du Pont de Nemours that "there is not a man in the U. S. who is not satisfied of the depth of his guilt."

The president's most serious difficulties during his second term, however, did not originate with traitors at home so much as with enemies abroad. Hardly had Jefferson been inaugurated before relations with England, and also with France and Spain, assumed serious dimensions. Two empires—the British and the French—were locked in a mortal struggle for world supremacy. Both being naval powers, they tried to strangle each other by blockade and counterblockade: neither the rights of neutrals nor international law were observed by the belligerents, and the neutrals were bound to suffer as well as profit by their privileged situation. Facing the two leviathans, as Jefferson called them, across the Atlantic Ocean was the United States; depending upon salt water transportation for its imports and exports, it too was a marine power—although not a significant naval one. The navy, which had been reduced to a minimum under Gallatin's policy of economy, was weak and ineffective against the depredations from Anglo-French predators against American shipping and American rights.

As America suffered deep humiliations at sea, Jefferson directed the course of foreign affairs by a policy of enlightened self-interest. He was firm in his unwillingness to favor and help Napoleon's ambitious schemes in any way by declaring war against England; but, on the other hand, the prospect of forming a de facto alliance with a country which had by tradition deliberately insulted and manifestly entertained feelings of scorn and distrust toward the young republic was equally abhorrent to him. Repeated insults against national honor and pride arouse the national spirit, but Jefferson, who loved peace, by keeping this country out of the deadly conflict in which Europe was engaged was able to lay the solid foundations of unparalleled prosperity. While farms and factories of the Old World were abandoned and the young manhood of Europe perished on the battlefields, new industries were developed and immense territories were put under cultivation in this country as the population grew at a truly remarkable rate from 5,300,000 in 1800 to over 7,250,000 in 1810. When, after the embargo and Waterloo, Europe resumed her peaceful pursuits, it was found that Jefferson's policies in the pursuit of peace had their rewards: the whole life of the nation was quickened, the industrial revolution hastened, and America freed herself of economic dependence on the Old World.

Although peace remained the ultimate ideal of the United States, Jefferson's annual message of December 1805 had to present very "unpleasant views of violence and wrong." There were circumstances which admitted of no peaceful remedy; some evils were "of a nature to be met by force only, & all of them may lead to it." England ruled the waves and was undisputed mistress of the ocean, having annihilated Napoleon's sea power at the battle of Trafalgar on October 21, 1805. She could now suspend rules of international law and enforce her own regulations as she pleased, and she proceeded to do so. She now set herself to ruin the American carrying trade, which in recent years had come to be almost the only means of communication between the nations of Europe and their colonial dependencies. Seizure and confiscation, impressment and blockade in all waters became the order of the day. Seafaring and commercial citizens of the Atlantic seaboard were infuriated and humiliated, in particular, with the British policy of impressment of American sailors on the high seas. Being engaged in a desperate fight with the conqueror of Europe, the British were frequently shorthanded of sailors in a war in which naval power played a dominant role. To recruit their navy, the British therefore resorted to the brutal and degrading practice of seizing and abducting any sailor off an American ship, on the pretext that they were British warships. In the midst of the rising tension Jefferson addressed Congress in December 1805:

Our coasts have been infested, and our harbors watched by private armed vessels, some of them without commissions, some with legal commissions, others with those of legal form, but committing piratical acts beyond the authority of their commissions. They have captured in the very entrance of our harbors, as well as on the high seas, not only the vessels of our friends coming to trade with us, but our own also. They have carried them off under pretence of legal adjudication, but not daring to approach a court of justice, they have plundered & sunk them by the way, or in obscure places, where no evidence could arise against them, maltreating the crews, & abandoning them in boats in the open sea, or on desert shores, without food or covering. These enormities appearing to be unreached by any control of their sovereigns, I found it necessary to equip a force, to cruise within our own seas, to arrest all vessels of these descriptions found hovering on our coasts, within the limits of the Gulf stream, and to bring the offenders in for trial as pirates.

The most exasperating and humiliating case of impressment occurred in June 1807 when the American frigate Chesapeake *of thirty-eight guns was hailed by the British man-of-war* Leopard *of fifty guns outside the capes at Norfolk. The* Leopard *demanded permission to search the American frigate for deserters; when the American commander refused, the British opened fire, killing three members of the crew and wounding eighteen. She was severely crippled and was searched; finally, with difficulty, she made her way back to Hampton Roads. The news of the attack on the* Chesapeake *provoked a burst of anger throughout the land. Resisting the clamor, Jefferson resorted to his favorite weapons of diplomacy and economic coercion, and demanded reparations and the end of impressments.*

Before the nation could recover from this scandalous blow, her commerce was caught between the hammer and the anvil, between the British blockade of France and the French counterblockade of Britain. In retaliation against Napoleon's Berlin decree at the end of November 1806—placing the British islands in a state of blockade, declaring all merchandise coming from England subject to confiscation, and refusing admission into any French port to any vessel coming from England or her colonies—the British issued Orders in Council in November 1807, declaring that all European ports that excluded the British should henceforth be "subject to the same restrictions." Forbidden by England to trade with France, and by France to trade with England, neutral shipping in general and American shipping in particular were now caught in a crushing dilemma. The repeated outrages and contemptuous violations of "the sea pirates and land robbers of Europe," as Jefferson appropriately designated the two belligerents, threatened to drive American commerce from the ocean or to force her into war with both powers.

Was there no substitute for war? Jefferson was convinced there was. The philosopher-president and apostle of peace answered these edicts with an economic embargo, passed overwhelmingly by Congress in December 1807 despite the opposition of New England Federalists and some dissentient Republicans. By recommending an embargo policy, his principal object was to exert increasing pressure on the commercial misery of Europe and thereby hasten the end of the war. The situation, as he saw it in December 1807, was stated frankly to a correspondent:

The whole world is laid under interdict by these two nations, and our vessels, their cargoes, and crews, are to be taken by the one or the other for whatever place they may be destined out of our own limits. If therefore, on leaving our harbours, we are certainly to lose them, is it not better for the vessels, cargoes, and seamen, to keep them at home?

French foreign office, Paris.

The embargo was a bold experiment in self-sacrificing economic coercion, a trial of national endurance, by which American vessels were prohibited from sailing for foreign ports and were confined to coasting trade, while foreign vessels were prohibited from taking out cargoes from American ports. The embargo, as Jefferson pointed out, was no new policy and no new measure; it was simply a recognition of a situation created by both France and Great Britain. "The alternative was between that and war," Jefferson wrote in March 1808, "and in fact it is the last card we have to play, short of war." At the same time a nonimportation law went into force, by which British and French manufactures were excluded. The idea behind these dual measures —embargo and nonimportation—was excellent, but the success of both depended on two assumptions: one was that the embargo could be enforced, and the other was that Britain's trade with the United States was of such importance that its restriction would gravely damage her economy and cripple her military position. On both assumptions Jefferson miscalculated badly.

The embargo soon became worse than futile as shipowners and merchants turned to system-

atic smuggling and began to realize sizeable profits from illegal trading. Small businesses and the little folk—farmers, traders, and artisans—were hit severely and became the chief sufferers of Jefferson's measures. Ports were idle, ships dismantled, bankruptcies multiplied, and discontent spread. The distress in the country was not only visible but vocal, particularly from New England—a region that suffered most under the embargo, owing to its commercial economy. A typical letter from New England, addressed to President Jefferson, read: "You Infernal Villain, How much longer are you going to keep this damned Embargo on to starve us poor people." He suffered from "the peltings of the storm" and wrote pathetically to Benjamin Rush: "Oh! for the day when I shall be withdrawn from it; when I shall have leisure to enjoy my family, my friends, my farm and books." At no time during his long political career were his motives less partisan and more zealously nationalistic; at no time, either, was he more bitterly attacked.

But the defection of his own Republicans in Congress, the divergence of opinion in his Cabinet, the anonymous letters and press campaign launched against him had no power to shake his resolution to carry out his policy. Although the embargo was violently opposed and widely evaded, particularly by the Federalist merchants of New England, he hoped that the "present paroxysm of the insanity of Europe," as he called it, would cease in time and that, regardless of provocations, he would be able to keep America out of the war. "In truth I consider Europe but as a great mad house, & in the present deranged state of their moral faculties to be pitied and avoided," he wrote David Bailey Warden. "There is no bravery in fighting a maniac." To John Langdon he wrote in August 1808: "I think one war enough for the life of one man: and you and I have gone through one which at least may lessen our impatience to embark in another."

Jefferson never considered the embargo as a permanent policy, but rather as a political expedient and experiment, a last alternative to war. As early as March 1808, he wrote to Charles Pinckney, the former envoy to Spain, that the effect of the embargo would be "to postpone for this year the immediate danger of a rupture with England." He admitted that a time would come "when war would be preferable to a continuance of the embargo and that the question would have to be decided at the next meeting of Congress unless peace intervened in the meantime." The last annual message of Jefferson to Congress in November 1808 was noncommittal on the measures to be taken; the decision was left to Congress. He was quite deliberate in his efforts to maintain a reserved attitude during the remainder of his term, and after the election he followed a policy of not proposing measures which his successor would have to execute:

I have thought it right to take no part myself in proposing measures, the execution of which will devolve on my successor. I am therefore chiefly an unmedling listener to what others say.

But he was, nonetheless, caught by surprise when Congress moved suddenly to repeal the embargo:

I thought Congress had taken their ground firmly for continuing their embargo till June, and then war. But a sudden and unaccountable revolution of opinion took place the last week, chiefly among the New England and New York members, and in a kind of panic they voted the 4th of March for removing the embargo, and by such a majority as gave all reason to believe they would not agree either to war or non-intercourse. This, too, was after we had become satisfied that the Essex Junto had found their expectation desperate, of inducing the people there to either separation or forcible opposition. The majority of Congress, however, has now rallied to the removing the embargo on the 4th of March, non-intercourse with *France* and *Great Britain*, trade everywhere else, and continuing war preparations.

Jefferson protested to the last that if the suspension of commerce had been complete and the embargo steadfastly adhered to, American shipping would have been restored to its rights without war.

On March 4, 1809, Jefferson ended his eight years in the presidency and transferred the executive power to his friend and disciple, James Madison. He was bitterly disappointed at the miscarriage of his favorite theory of economic independence and isolation from Europe and the necessity of preserving peace at any cost. The embargo had forced the country

into measures which had threatened its dissolution and brought down great financial distress and a debilitating depression upon the whole nation; his own party was compelled virtually to acknowledge its failure by abandoning it. Jefferson's last days in Washington were clouded with burdens and bitterness, defiance and disobedience from Federalists and Republicans alike. Always keenly sensitive to the petty barbs and slanderous criticism directed at him by a resentful Senate, he thought increasingly about retirement and Monticello.

On March 11th, after arranging his affairs and packing his bags, he left Washington, never to return. Soon after he arrived at Monticello his neighbors in Albemarle County gave him a rousing welcome home; the former president was moved to tears as he addressed them:

Of you, then, my neighbors, I may ask, in the face of the world, "whose ox have I taken, or whom have I defrauded? Whom have I oppressed, or of whose hand have I received a bribe to blind mine eyes therewith?" On your verdict I rest.

"All my wishes end, where I hope my days will end, at Monticello."

CHAPTER XVII

THE SAGE OF MONTICELLO (1809–1826)

On *March 4, 1809, Jefferson transferred the power and duties of the presidency to his trusted successor James Madison. He declined an invitation to ride with Madison in a carriage to the Capitol, choosing rather to ride quietly unattended to the inauguration: "I wished not to divide with him the honors of the day," he said. "It pleased me better to see them all bestowed on him." At last Jefferson could look forward to the seventeen years of tranquil private life which were left to him—years filled with the varied, bristling activities of a mind that never lost its zestful curiosity, its wide versatility, nor its sharp edge of discrimination. He was drawn irresistibly to his books, his family, his acres, his buildings, his gardens, his undisturbed mornings of study and letter writing, and his relaxed hours with a host of devoted friends and welcome guests. It had long been his fervent wish to retire to the bucolic pleasures of Monticello; he wrote with profound pathos to Dupont de Nemours:*

Never did a prisoner, released from his chains, feel such relief as I shall on shaking off the shackles of power. Nature intended me for the tranquil pursuits of science, by rendering them my supreme delight. But the enormities of the times in which I have lived, have forced me to take a part in resisting them, and to commit myself on the boisterous ocean of political passions. I thank God for the opportunity of retiring from them without censure, and carrying with me the most consoling proofs of public approbation.

His whole life, though full and fruitful, had been a dynamic conflict between private inclination and public duty. But now he was within a month of his sixty-sixth birthday, and after forty years of public service, during which he had experienced some defeats and many triumphs, his name was imperishably linked with the history of the nation. By means of peace and persuasion he had doubled the territory of the United States and had pulled together, from loose and scattered materials, a powerful political party. His ideals of liberty were written into the law of the land and had permanently enshrined his name as the prophet of radical democracy. And yet "I have the consolation to reflect," he wrote in 1818, "that during the period of my administration not a drop of the blood of a single fellow citizen was shed by the sword of war or of the law."

Upon his final return to Monticello, he was a balanced and harmonious man with an immense reservoir of moral strength; he could face the opinion of his contemporaries and the judgment of history with detached compassion and serene wisdom. And so, returning to private life and the tranquillity of scientific and literary pursuits, he became a symbol of national unity and wise counsel, the Sage of Monticello. Both Madison and Monroe consulted him frequently for his advice on every important crisis during their administrations. To a younger generation of Americans the oracle of Monticello—the author of the Declaration of Independence and close friend of the now revered Washington—was a piece from the tapestry of American history.

On reaching Monticello Jefferson at once set about picking up the sadly raveled odds and ends of his farm work: restoring his neglected fields, directing domestic manufactures, building terraced gardens, and indulging his extravagant passion for architecture at Monticello and Poplar Forest, his new octagonal brick cottage in Bedford County. "All my wishes end, where I hope my days will end, at Monticello," he had once said to a friend; "Too many scenes of happiness mingle themselves with all the recollections of my native woods and feilds, to suffer them to be supplanted in my affection by any other." Monticello was really never finished; possibly it was never meant to be finished, but to serve as a kind of standing challenge to the ingenuity of its owner. "So I hope it will remain during my life," he is reported to have told a visitor, "as architecture is my delight, and putting up and pulling down, one of my favourite amusements." The congenial task of gardening appealed to him, in particular:

No occupation is so delightful to me as the culture of the earth, and no culture comparable to that of the garden. Such a variety of subjects, some one always coming to perfection, the failure of one thing repaired by the success of another, and instead of one harvest a continued one through the year. Under a total want of demand except for our family table, I am still devoted to the garden. But though an old man, I am but a young gardener.

In a letter to General Kosciusko, written in February 1810, he gave the best expression of the routine of his life at Monticello, which was by then a little world in itself with its nail factory and cotton mill, smithy and furniture shop.

I am retired to Monticello, where, in the bosom of my family and surrounded by my books, I enjoy a repose to which I have been long a stranger. My mornings are devoted to correspondence. From breakfast to dinner, I am in my shops, my garden, or on horseback among my farms; from dinner to dark, I give to society and recreation with my neighbors and friends; and from candle light to early bedtime, I read. My health is perfect; and my strength considerably re-enforced by the activity of the course I pursue. Perhaps it is as great as usually falls to the lot of near sixty-seven years of age. I talk of plows and harrows, of seeding and harvesting, with my neighbors, and of politics, too, if they choose, with as little reserve as the rest of my fellow citizens, and feel at length the blessing of being free to say and do what I please, without being responsible for it to any mortal. A part of my occupation, and by no means the least pleasing, is the direction of the studies of such young men as ask it. They place themselves in the neighboring village and have the use of my library and counsel and make a part of my society. In advising the course of their reading, I endeavor to keep their attention fixed on the main objects of all science, the freedom and happiness of man.

Jefferson's library suite at Monticello, with a plaster bust of John Adams by Binon.

The world would not—it could not—leave Jefferson alone in his retirement. Politicians, scientists, educators, doctors, economists, distinguished thinkers, and men of letters asked for his opinions and he continued quite happily his voluminous, spirited contacts with them. He was, he said, "devoured by correspondences," yet he was drawn irresistibly to the labor of letter writing. No letter remained unanswered. He frequently complained about the time consumed in maintaining his ever-widening cor-

respondence, but he could not resist an intellectual challenge or turn down an appeal for his advice or opinion. He was released from the close scrutiny of the public and the "cannibal press"; now, finally, he could express himself freely to a few chosen friends, revealing fully his intimate thoughts and communicating his hopes and doubts, his convictions and hatreds, without fear of being betrayed. These superb letters—among them essays and short treatises on every possible subject and numbering into the thousands—were written with zest and frankness, with impetuousness and particular fullness on a number of subjects close to his heart; they reveal a mind that was still fresh, often provocative, and untrammeled. Although Jefferson complained that "the decays of age had enfeebled the useful energies of the mind" and that he was only "an old half-strung fiddle" as he advanced in age, he kept, practically to his last day, his alertness, his encyclopedic curiosity, and an extraordinary capacity for work.

Jefferson's old age is a remarkable proof of the observation made by his daughter Martha that her father had never forsaken a friend or a principle. Age and experience had only enlarged his progressive outlook, widened his circle of friendships, and deepened his democratic faith. Nothing pleased him more than the resumption at the beginning of 1812 of his old friendship with John Adams, their earlier political differences having been reconciled through the efforts of their common friend, Dr. Benjamin Rush of Philadelphia. They had not been on speaking terms since Adams' sulky departure from Washington on the morning of March 4, 1801, following his unseemly effort to confine the incoming administration by packing the federal courts. But time had blunted the sharp edges of their political differences, and now that both were in retirement, the two old friends resumed a correspondence that was to end only with their deaths. Jefferson was deeply moved when he heard indirectly that during a conversation Adams had mentioned his name, adding: "I always loved Jefferson, and still love him." "This is enough for me," Jefferson wrote Rush, and now awaited only an "occasion to express to Mr. Adams my unchanged affections for him."

The stone barn at Bremo.

*Monticello, Albemarle County, near Charlottesville, Virginia,
was Jefferson's own creation. With it he developed a new American architectural style,
romantic classicism. No other house in America so well reflects the personality
of its builder and owner.*

*Jefferson's bedroom and library at Monticello. This apartment
where he slept, read, and wrote was his sanctum sanctorum.
The bed, designed by Jefferson, is in an alcove open on both sides.*

Adams took the initial step, sending to Jefferson "two Pieces of Homespun lately produced in this quarter," which were nothing less than two stout volumes of John Quincy Adams' Lectures on Rhetoric and Oratory delivered when he was Boylston Professor at Harvard College. In a letter filled with eagerness and warmth, Jefferson replied:

A letter from you calls up recollections very dear to my mind. It carries me back to the times when, beset with difficulties and dangers, we were fellow laborers in the same cause, struggling for what is most valuable to man, his right of self-government. . . . Of the signers of the Declaration of Independence I see now living not more than half a dozen on your side of the Potomak, and, on this side, myself alone. You and I have been wonderfully spared, and myself with remarkable

health, and a considerable activity of body and mind. I am on horseback 3. or 4. hours of every day; visit 3. or 4. times a year a possession I have 90 miles distant, performing the winter journey on horseback. I walk little however; a single mile being too much for me; and I live in the midst of my grandchildren, one of whom has lately promoted me to be a great grandfather. I have heard with pleasure that you also retain good health, and a greater power of exercise in walking than I do. But I would rather have heard this from yourself, and that, writing a letter, like mine, full of egotisms, and of details of your health, your habits, occupations and enjoyments, I should have the pleasure of knowing that, in the race of life, you do not keep, in it's physical decline, the same distance ahead of me which you have done in political honors and atchievements. No circumstances have lessened the interest I feel in

Bremo—considered the most perfect expression of the Jeffersonian tradition—after designs by General John Hartwell Cocke and John Neilson, which Jefferson approved.

The Rotunda, University of Virginia, Charlottesville.

these particulars respecting yourself; none have suspended for one moment my sincere esteem for you; and I now salute you with unchanged affections and respect.

This letter inaugurated a series of over one hundred and fifty communications between Monticello and Quincy that are remarkable for their brilliant, bold adventuring into the realm of ideas. The two old gentlemen, out of their massive learning and vast intellectual curiosity, wrote on every conceivable subject, from classical authors to contour farming. One of their debates involved the perplexing riddle of life and death. "Would you go back to your Cradle and live over again Your 70 Years?" Adams asked Jefferson. "I hesitate to say," Jefferson replied:

From 25. to 60., I would say Yes; and might go further back, but not come lower down. For, at the latter period, with most of us, the powers of life are sensibly on the wane, sight becomes dim, hearing dull, memory constantly enlarging it's frightful blank and parting with all we have ever seen or known, spirits evaporate, bodily debility creeps on palsying every limb, and so faculty after faculty quits us, and where then is life?

In October 1823, when Jefferson had passed his eightieth birthday, he wrote to Adams with enthusiasm of his last great undertaking, the founding and building of the University of Virginia:

Crippled wrists and fingers make writing slow and laborious. But, while writing to you, I lose the sense of these things, in the recollection of antient times, when youth and health made happiness out of every thing. I forget for a while the hoary winter of age, when we can think of nothing but how to keep ourselves warm, and how to get rid of our heavy hours until the friendly hand of death shall rid us of all at once. Against this tedium vitae however I am fortunately mounted on a Hobby, which indeed I should have better managed some 30. or 40. years ago, but whose easy amble is still sufficient to give exercise and amusement to an Octogenary rider. This is the establishment of an University, on a scale more comprehensive, and in a country more healthy and central than our old William and Mary.

In spite of his advanced age, Jefferson now launched an ambitious—many people thought visionary—plan for public education in the democracy and gave the last years of his life and labors to its realization. He had long pondered on the subject of universal education and consistently maintained that "the most effectual means of preventing the perversion of power into tyranny are to illuminate so far as possible the minds of the people." He had no doubt that "if a nation expects to be ignorant and free . . . it expects what never was and never will be." Neither the Assembly nor the public was prepared for such a comprehensive scheme of education, and when it was first introduced, it was, as Jefferson expected, rejected. Legislators, he observed dryly, "do not generally possess information enough to perceive the important truths, that knolege is happiness."

Finally, however, early in 1818 the Virginia legislature, stimulated by the force of a considerable private subscription, appropriated the generous sum of $15,000 for the endowment and support of a university. For the next six years Jefferson lived and breathed only for the university: he was its architect; he superintended every detail of its planning and construction; he laid down its lines of organiza-

The pavilions for the professors, separated by rooms for students, University of Virginia, with "a small and separate lodge

tion and educational policy; he fought for legislative funds necessary to carry it to completion; and he directed the assembling of its faculty. "This institution of my native state, the Hobby of my old age," he wrote Destutt de Tracy in 1820, "will be based on the illimitable freedom of the human mind, to explore and to expose every subject susceptible of it's contemplation." His greatest difficulty in building the college, however, was financial, because the cost of construction so far exceeded all estimates and expectations. Bit by bit the money was grudgingly voted by the legislature; by the time the construction on the principal buildings was completed, Jefferson had spent $300,000 in state appropriations.

The University of Virginia, set amid two hundred fifty acres of high ground in Char-

for each professorship, with only a hall below for his class, and two chambers above for himself."

lottesville and commanding a superb prospect, made a powerful impression on visitors. To Nathaniel Bowditch, Jefferson explained the arrangement of the pavilions:

The plan of building is not to erect one single magnificent building to contain everybody and everything, but to make of it an academical village in which every professor should have his separate house, containing his lecturing room with two, three, or four rooms for his own accommodation according as he may have a family or no family, with kitchen, garden, etc.; distinct dormitories for the students, not more than two in a room; and separate boarding houses for dieting them by private housekeepers. We concluded to employ no professor who is not of the first order of the

North Range student quarters, University of Virginia, expressing Jefferson's idea of building a university in the form "of an academical village rather than of one large building."

science he professes, that when we can find such in our own country we shall prefer them and when we cannot we will procure them wherever else to be found.

The university—which finally opened in 1825, the winter before his death—was the last great task to which Jefferson put his hand. It was an achievement of which he was no less proud than of having written the Declaration of Independence.

Despite this preoccupation during these last years, however, Jefferson continued to pursue a multitude of other tasks. In his eightieth year, when President Monroe asked his advice on the grave international matter of cooperating with Great Britain to keep European powers out of the Americas, Jefferson wrote long expositions with singular energy on hemispheric politics. Amazed at and pleased with Britain's offer of an alliance to keep European powers out of the Western Hemisphere, Jefferson, an astute practitioner of realpolitik in spite of his theoretical isolationism, urged immediate acceptance:

The question presented by the letters you have sent me, is the most momentous which has ever been offered to my contemplation since that of Independence. That made us a

182

nation, this sets our compass and points the course which we are to steer through the ocean of time opening on us. And never could we embark on it under circumstances more auspicious. Our first and fundamental maxim should be, never to entangle ourselves in the broils of Europe. Our second, never to suffer Europe to intermeddle with cis-Atlantic affairs.

Monroe accepted Jefferson's advice and sent a message to Congress, announcing that this country would declare any attempt of European powers "to extend their systems to any portion of this hemisphere as dangerous to our peace and safety." Thus, fathered by Jefferson, was born the Monroe Doctrine.

Jefferson's "long and serene day," now drawing to a close, was clouded by financial disaster and the threat of bankruptcy. He was subjected to demands of the most extensive hospitality that the young nation had ever seen, and no estate could for long stand such a persistent financial drain upon it. As one of the few surviving Founding Fathers, he became a legend in his own lifetime. Biographers besieged him for materials to write his life, artists and sculptors were commissioned to paint and carve him, and the visitors who invaded Monticello to see "the Immortal Jefferson" became so constant and so great that in the end they practically ate him out of house and home. To maintain what amounted to a virtual hotel and to support his large family of grandchildren and all manner of kinsfolk, he had to resort to borrowing. To this were added the disastrous financial consequences of the War of 1812 and the panic and depression of 1819. He had, moreover, frequently advanced money to friends who thought themselves more hard-pressed than he, and occasionally he was forced to make good on their notes. This left

him a ruined man. His grandson Thomas Jefferson Randolph quoted him as saying, as early as 1814, that "if he lived long enough he would beggar his family, that the number of persons he was compelled to entertain would devour his estate; many bringing letters from his ancient friends, and all coming with respectful feelings—he could not shut his door in their faces." Despite the magnificent architectural appearance of Monticello and the generous hospitality Jefferson practiced there, evidence of poverty was increasingly visible to visitors. "The first thing which attracted our attention," wrote Francis Calley Gray, who visited Monticello in the winter of 1814, "was the state of the chairs. They had leather bottoms stuffed with hair, but the bottoms were completely worn through and the hair sticking out in all directions."

As time went on, Jefferson's visits to Poplar Forest, usually with several of his granddaughters, took on the nature of a retreat from the swarm of visitors at Monticello. He was, nevertheless, still filled with a zest for living. There were so many things to do, such as measuring the high Peaks of Otter, which were visible from Poplar Forest:

When lately measuring trigonometrically the height of the Peaks of Otter . . . my object was only to gratify a common curiosity as to the height of those mountains, which we deem our highest. . . . The ridge of mountains of which Monticello is one, is generally low; there is one in it, however, called Peter's Mountain, considerably higher than the general ridge. This being within a dozen miles of me, northeastwardly, I think in the spring of the year to measure it . . . which may serve as another trial of the logarithmic theory.

To raise money, Jefferson was ultimately

Peaks of Otter in winter.

driven to deprive himself of the things he most cherished—his books. He had thought of leaving his library to the University of Virginia, but when in August 1814 the British set fire to the Capitol, the Congressional Library was almost totally destroyed. A few weeks later Jefferson offered his personal library to Congress on such terms as they might choose to offer:

You know my collection, its condition and extent. I have been fifty years making it, and have spared no pains, opportunity or expense, to make it what it is. While residing in Paris, I devoted every afternoon I was disengaged, for a summer or two, in examining all the principal bookstores, turning over every book with my own hand, and putting by everything which related to America, and indeed whatever was rare and valuable in every science. Besides this, I had standing orders during the whole time I was in Europe, on its principal book-marts. . . . During the same period, and after my return to America, I was led to procure, also, whatever related to the duties of those in the high concerns of the nation. So that the collection, which I suppose is of between nine and ten thousand volumes, while it includes what is chiefly valuable in science and

literature generally, extends more particularly to whatever belongs to the American statesman.

In October the offer was laid before the Senate, where political opponents began at once to raise objections: some complained that many of the books were in foreign languages and therefore useless to the average reader; others objected that it contained works of an atheistical and immoral character, which might corrupt Congress; and one member insisted that the works of Voltaire, Rousseau, and Locke should be returned to the owner. Finally, in

January 1815, after much wrangling, Congress agreed to purchase the major portion of the collection of 6,500 volumes for $23,950. It was a mean offer, for the original cost was more than double this amount, but Jefferson accepted it without a murmur. The money was a godsend, even though he was able to keep only about one third of it: the remainder went immediately to his creditors.

As the old patriarch's life was drawing to a close, the future of his large debt-ridden family of grandchildren was a constant vexation to him. With intense mortification, he wrote Madison in February 1826 proposing the idea of selling off with the permission of the state legislature enough of his property to satisfy his pressing debts. "If refused," he warned Madison, "I must sell everything here, perhaps considerably in Bedford, move thither with my family, where I have not even a log hut to put my head into, and whether ground for burial, will depend on the depredations which, under the form of sales, shall have been committed on my property." He begged his old friend's pardon for troubling him:

But why afflict you with these details? Indeed, I cannot tell, unless pains are lessened by communication with a friend. The friendship which has subsisted between us, now half a century, and the harmony of our political principles and pursuits, have been sources of constant happiness to me through that long period. . . . It has . . . been a great solace to me, to believe that you are engaged in vindicating to posterity the course we have pursued for preserving to them, in all their purity, the blessings of self-government, which we had assisted too in acquiring for them. If ever the earth has beheld a system of administration conducted with a single and steadfast eye to the general interest and happiness of those committed to it, one which, protected by truth, can never know reproach, it is that to which our lives have been devoted.

This was a farewell letter—the last time Jefferson communicated with Madison.

When news reached the outside world that the author of the Declaration of Independence, the most famous republican statesman of his time, was in dire straits, mass meetings were held all over the nation—North and South— where spontaneous sums were raised by popular subscription and promptly forwarded to him. The old ailing patriot was not only grateful, but proud of his countrymen: "No cent of this," he said with tears in his eyes, "is wrung from the taxpayer. It is a pure and unsolicited offering of love." It was a vindication of his lifelong belief in the goodness of the people and his devotion to their cause.

Through the spring of 1826, Jefferson's health failed rapidly. In order not to alarm his family, he tried to be up and about, and even to ride for a short time, but he knew he was dying. In the middle of March he drew up his will. As June wore on, life began to ebb and the strength still left in his once powerful frame declined, although his mind retained its keen force and clearness throughout, and his speech, according to visitors, was as vigorous and animated as usual.

Adams and Jefferson continued their correspondence to within three months of their deaths. It lapsed on a pleasant note. Jefferson's favorite grandson and namesake, Thomas Jefferson Randolph, was making a trip to Boston, which he could not consider complete without visiting Mr. Adams at Quincy. He delivered Jefferson's last letter to Adams. It "has been a cordial to me," came the reply from Adams, whose valedictory had been: "We shall meet again, so wishes and so believes your friend, but if we are disappointed we shall never know it."

Too feeble to accept invitations to celebrations of the fiftieth anniversary of the Declaration of Independence on the Fourth of July, both anticipated the spirit of the forthcoming occasion with a reply. Adams provided the citizens of Quincy at their request with a toast: "Independence forever!" An invitation came to Jefferson to attend the function at Washington. It moved him deeply; he was conscious of the significance of the approaching ceremony as were few others in America. Of all the fifty-six signers, only he and Adams and

Charles Carroll were still alive after the passage of a half-century. He therefore wrote the mayor of Washington on June 24th, expressing his real disappointment that he was old and ill, and would be unable to celebrate the day with the citizens of that city. His reply was a singularly brilliant formulation, an outburst, of his democratic faith—one of the most forceful that he ever made. It was also the last letter he ever wrote:

May it be to the world, what I believe it will be (to some parts sooner, to others later, but finally to all,) the signal of arousing men to burst the chains under which monkish ignorance and superstition had persuaded them to bind themselves, and to assume the blessings and security of self-government. That form which we have substituted, restores the free right to the unbounded exercise of reason and freedom of opinion. All eyes are opened, or

Jefferson's own books, now in the Library of Congress.

opening, to the rights of man. The general spread of the light of science has already laid open to every view the palpable truth, that the mass of mankind has not been born with saddles on their backs, nor a favored few booted and spurred, ready to ride them legitimately, by the grace of God. These are grounds of hope for others. For ourselves, let the annual return of this day forever refresh our recollections of these rights, and an undiminished devotion to them.

On July 2 Jefferson called in his family for a final farewell, which "was calm and composed," according to his grandson Thomas Jefferson Randolph, "impressing admonitions upon them, the cardinal points of which were, to pursue virtue, be true and truthful." He slept through the night, and when he awoke he remarked: "This is the fourth of July." It was only the third. He was fighting with every ounce of his weak energy to live until the day of jubilee. As he grew weaker, it became evident that his mind was being revisited by events of a half-century earlier. The night of the third was disturbed and partly delirious: "he sat up in his sleep and went through all the forms of writing; spoke of the Committee of Safety, saying it ought to be warned." At eleven o'clock the next morning his lips moved faintly and then the sick man lost consciousness.

Death came quietly and painlessly to Thomas Jefferson about two hours later, at ten minutes to one, on July 4, 1826—fifty years, to the day, after the signing of the Declaration of Independence. At that moment, across the length and breadth of the United States, hundreds of thousands of Americans were listening to Fourth of July orations. In thousands of towns, church bells were tolling and cannon were booming in the celebration of freedom and independence. Also at that moment, in Quincy, Massachusetts, his old friend and fellow John Adams was dying. About five hours later, at sunset on the same day, Adams passed away. His last recorded words were "Thomas Jefferson still survives."

Monticello from Shadwell.

BIBLIOGRAPHY

THIS IS a selective bibliography covering only the works cited by short titles below. In the references, the first numbers given are those of the pages of this book; first words of the quotation follow, then the source, volume, and page number.

Adams—*The Works of John Adams, Second President of the United States: with a Life of the Author*, ed. Charles Francis Adams, Boston, 1850-1856; 10 vols.

Adams Diary—*Diary and Autobiography of John Adams*, ed. L. H. Butterfield, Cambridge, 1961; 4 vols.

Bowers—Claude G. Bowers, *The Young Jefferson, 1743-1789*, Boston, 1945.

Boyd—*The Papers of Thomas Jefferson*, ed. Julian P. Boyd, Princeton, 1950- ; 17 vols. to date.

Cappon—*The Adams-Jefferson Letters: The Complete Correspondence Between Thomas Jefferson and Abigail and John Adams*, ed. Lester J. Cappon, Chapel Hill, 1959; 2 vols.

Chastellux—Marquis de Chastellux, *Travels in North America in the Years 1780, 1781 and 1782*, ed. Howard C. Rice Jr., Chapel Hill, 1963; 2 vols.

Chinard—Gilbert Chinard, *Thomas Jefferson, The Apostle of Americanism*, Boston, 1943.

Domestic Life—Sarah N. Randolph, *The Domestic Life of Thomas Jefferson Compiled from Family Letters and Reminiscences*, New York, 1871.

Ford—*The Writings of Thomas Jefferson*, ed. Paul Leicester Ford, "Letterpress Edition," New York, 1892-1899; 10 vols.

Forman—S. E. Forman, *The Life and Writings of Thomas Jefferson*, Indianapolis, 1900.

Hirst—Francis W. Hirst, *Life and Letters of Thomas Jefferson*, New York, 1926.

Kimball—Marie Kimball, *Jefferson, The Scene of Europe, 1784-1789*, New York, 1950.

Mayo—*Jefferson Himself; The Personal Narrative of a Many-Sided American*, ed. Bernard Mayo, Boston, 1942.

Nock—Albert Jay Nock, *Jefferson*, Washington, 1926.

Notes on Va.—Thomas Jefferson, *Notes on the State of Virginia*, ed. William Peden, Chapel Hill, 1955.

Padover, *Complete*—*The Complete Jefferson, Containing His Major Writings, Published and Unpublished, Except His Letters*, ed. Saul K. Padover, New York, 1943.

Padover, *Jefferson*—Saul K. Padover, *Jefferson*, New York, 1942.

Padover, *Profile*—*A Jefferson Profile, As Revealed in His Letters*, ed. Saul K. Padover, New York, 1956.

Peterson—*Thomas Jefferson, A Profile*, ed. Merrill D. Peterson, New York, 1967.

Rosenberger—*Jefferson Reader: A Treasury of Writings About Thomas Jefferson*, ed. Francis Coleman Rosenberger, New York, 1953.

Schachner—Nathan Schachner, *Thomas Jefferson, A Biography*, New York, 1960; 3rd printing, one vol. edn.

Wise—*Thomas Jefferson, Then and Now, 1743-1943*, ed. James Waterman Wise, New York, 1943.

REFERENCES

Introduction
9. Thomas Jefferson, Adams, 1:636.
9. is the most, Padover, *Profile*, xxiv.
9. The principles, Rosenberger, 236.
9. the people, Wise, 29.
9. The immortality, Rosenberger, 336.
10. He was, Peterson, x.
10. Jefferson was, Peterson, 53.
10. Almost every, Rosenberger, 11.
10. I have sworn, Ford, 7:460.

Chapter I
13. education had, Ford, 1:2.
13. whole care, *Domestic Life*, 26.
14. He placed, Ford, 1:3.
14. mouldy pies, Bowers, 12.
14. So much, Cappon, 2:307.
15. They trace, Ford, 1:2.
15. The tradition, Ford, 1:1.
16. to search, Boyd, 1:62.
17. Henry Weatherbourne's, Schachner, 9.
17. It was, *Domestic Life*, 22-23.
19. the various, *Domestic Life*, 26.
20. In the first, Boyd, 1:3.
20. From the circumstances, *Domestic Life*, 26.
22. rife with, Padover, *Jefferson*, 11.
22. No, if you, *Domestic Life*, 37.
23. I went, Ford, 1:3-4.
24. No man, Padover, *Complete*, 928.
24. Mr. Wythe, Ford, 1:4.
25. the ablest man, Ford, 1:4.
25. At these dinners, Padover, *Jefferson*, 14.
26. made any, Schachner, 30.
26. at ye billiard, Padover, *Jefferson*, 16.
27. In the most, Boyd, 1:11-12.
27. in the solid, Bowers, 29.
27. in pleading, Schachner, 33.
27. my second father, Schachner, 33.
27. In reading, Bowers, 32.
28. When I, Schachner, 35.
28. never knew, Padover, *Jefferson*, 22.

Chapter II
30. poem in, Bowers, 44.
30. My late loss, Boyd, 1:34-35.
32. which, like, Mayo, 25.
32. My friends, Schachner, 79.
32. with a lithe, *Domestic Life*, 43.
32. I must alter, Boyd, 1:71.
32. Offer prayers, Boyd, 1:78.
34. Our countrymen, Ford, 1:7.
34. Not thinking, Ford, 1:7-8, 9-12, 13.
36. set a pace, Forman, 11.
36. That these, Boyd, 1:134-135.
37. peculiar felicity, Mayo, 60.

Chapter III
39. to discountenance, Chinard, 54.
39. that it is, Hirst, 83.
39. Our brethren, Hirst, 84.
40. Ld. North's, Ford, 1:15-16.
40. calculate an eclipse, Forman, 13.
40. Mr. Jefferson came, Adams, 2:514n.
41. Our cause, Boyd, 1:217-218.
42. It was, Hirst, 92.
42. My mother, Schachner, 88.
42. I have never, Boyd, 1:252.
42. United Colonies, Forman, 16.
43. Every Post, Schachner, 117.
43. For God's sake, Boyd, 1:287.
43. such government, Schachner, 118-119.
43. On the 15th, Ford, 1:18-20, 21-22, 24-28.
45. When in, Boyd, 1:429-430.
46. In every stage, Boyd, 1:431-432.
48. As you justly, Schachner, 530.
48. Pickering's observations, Ford, 10:267.
48. not to find, Ford, 10:343.

Chapter IV
49. a full and free, Bowers, 162.
49. Our delegation, Ford, 1:48.
50. On the 11th, Ford, 1:48.
50. On the 12th, Ford, 1:49-50.
50. We had, Ford, 1:61-62.
51. The bill, Ford, 1:67-68.
52. We thought, Ford, 1:66, 67.
52. The bill, Ford, 1:62.
52. Well aware, Schachner, 159.
53. We the General, Boyd, 2:546-547.
54. I considered, Ford, 1:68-69.

Chapter V
55. It is a cruel, Boyd, 2:298.
56. The various calamities, Boyd, 3:93-94.
56. Our trade, Boyd, 3:5.
56. There is really, Boyd, 3:433.
58. I think, Boyd, 4:197.
59. That there, Boyd, 4:294.
59. to repair, Boyd, 4:295.
59. They marched, Boyd, 4:334.

59. Acquainted as, Boyd, 4:487.
60. The enemy, Boyd, 5:623.
61. In December, *Notes on Va.*, 126-127.
62. It has been, Boyd, 4:265.
62. I did not, Boyd, 13:363-364.
63. in the strongest, Padover, *Jefferson*, 101.
63. This house, Chastellux, 2:390-391.
65. walked almost, *Domestic Life*, 63.
65. Sept. 6, Schachner, 238.
65. There is a time, Chinard, 138.

Chapter VI
67. written in Virginia, *Notes on Va.*, 2.
67. The *Ohio, Notes on Va.*, 10.
67. will be one, *Notes on Va.*, 7.
68. The passage, *Notes on Va.*, 19.
68. The *Natural bridge, Notes on Va.*, 24-25.
68. this scene, Chinard, 121.
68. the animals, *Notes on Va.*, 47.
69. I may challenge, *Notes on Va.*, 62-63.
70. Those who labour, *Notes on Va.*, 164-165.
71. Young as we, *Notes on Va.*, 174-175.
71. one of America's, *Notes on Va.*, xxv.
72. The conviction that, Boyd, 6:359-360.
72. you were so, Boyd, 6:374.
72. The plan of, Boyd, 6:374.
73. I hope you, Boyd, 6:380.
73. Some ladies think, Boyd, 6:417.
74. stating the receipt, Ford, 1:77.
74. Our body was, Ford, 1:81.
75. they shall forever, Boyd, 6:608.

Chapter VII
77. I understand, Boyd, 7:400.
77. I thank you, Boyd, 8:230.
78. My duties, Ford, 1:90.
78. When he left, Ford, 5:292.
78. The succession, Ford, 5:293.
79. He is a great, Boyd, 11:95-96.
80. Behold me, Boyd, 8:568-569.
81. With respect, Boyd, 8:569.
81. In science, Boyd, 8:569.
81. Were I to proceed, Boyd, 8:569.
81. The property, Boyd, 8:682.
82. I am now, Boyd, 8:500.
82. I consider, Boyd, 8:239.
84. believe in, Nock, 91.
84. You are then, Boyd, 11:122-123.
84. I agree, Boyd, 11:392.
84. The arts, Boyd, 11:393.
84. Our good ladies, Nock, 93-94.
87. By having them, Boyd, 7:505.
87. There is a new, Boyd, 7:505.
88. Have you, Boyd, 8:462.
88. Two artists, Boyd, 8:599.
88. An improvement, Boyd, 8:455.
88. As you seem, Boyd, 13:379-381.
89. What a feild, Boyd, 14:699.
89. I was written, Ford, 1:63-64.
90. I send by, Boyd, 9:240.

Chapter VIII
91. to come here, Cappon, 1:123.
91. Mr. Adams, Boyd, 9:325.

91. carrying Rocks, Cappon, 1:131.
91. that money, Cappon, 1:133.
91. But what, Boyd, 9:468.
91. I acknolege, Cappon, 1:142-143.
92. some of, Kimball, 133.
92. Our conferences, Kimball, 134.
92. On my presentation, Ford, 1:89.
92. The King, Kimball, 135.
92. the distance, Ford, 1:89.
92. we afterwards, Nock, 107.
93. of all nations, Boyd, 12:193.
93. put an end, Boyd, 9:326.
93. The gardening, Boyd, 9:445.
93. Ridings, Parks, *Adams Diary*, 3:186.
93. I always walked, Boyd, 9:369.
93. The Octagonal dome, Boyd, 9:369.
95. The lake covers, Boyd, 9:370-371.
96. 15. men, Boyd, 9:371.
97. for seeing, Kimball, 149-150.
97. The water here, Boyd, 9:372.
98. our natural enemies, Kimball, 157.
98. find the affections, Boyd, 12:225.

Chapter IX
99. I am meditating, Cappon, 1:141.
100. Having performed, Boyd, 10:443-446.
100. I suppose you, Cappon, 1:146.
101. With regard, Cappon, 1:168.
101. The Beginnings, Boyd, 11:252.
101. I hold it, Boyd, 11:93.
101. The commotions, Boyd, 10:629.
101. The people, Boyd, 11:49.
102. In a former, Boyd, 11:96.
105. Here I am, Boyd, 11:226.
106. It was built, Boyd, 8:535.
106. in the opinion, Boyd, 8:538.
107. Here I am, Boyd, 11:226.
107. My journey, Boyd, 11:339-343.
108. I am now, Boyd, 11:247-248.
108. I had thought, Boyd, 11:254.
109. I am constantly, Boyd, 11:283.
110. I have often, Boyd, 11:285.
110. At Marseilles, Boyd, 11:287.
111. tolerably good, Boyd, 11:431.
111. this climate, Boyd, 11:287.
113. Fall down, Boyd, 13:272.
113. Further on, Boyd, 11:432-433.
114. The country, Boyd, 11:435.
114. From Vercelli, Boyd, 11:436.
114. I examined, Boyd, 11:437-438.
114. I set out, Boyd, 11:587.
115. I have passed, Boyd, 11:371-372.
116. cloudless skies, Boyd, 11:369.
116. The locks, Boyd, 11:446-447.

Chapter X
117. God forbid, Boyd, 12:356.
118. the vaunted scene, Boyd, 8:568.
118. The politics, Boyd, 9:264.
118. I like much, Boyd, 12:439-440.
119. I will now add, Boyd, 12:440.
120. The second, Boyd, 12:440-441.
120. I own, Boyd, 12:442.
120. Our government, Boyd, 13:378.
121. You say, Boyd, 14:650.
121. The operations, Boyd, 14:678.
122. such a spirit, Bowers, 420.

122. the discovery, Boyd, 12:36.
122. You say, Boyd, 14:420-421.
123. new claims, Ford, 1:118.
123. had it been, Kimball, 278.
123. The Noblesse, Ford, 1:129.
126. The Commons, Boyd, 15:196.
126. When they arrived, Ford, 1:145-146.
128. society & care, Ford, 1:148.
128. In a letter, Boyd, 15:118.
128. And here, Ford, 1:148-149.

Chapter XI
129. The federal, Boyd, 15:224.
129. kindly leaves, Boyd, 16:27-28.
129. no longer, Boyd, 16:184.
130. My daughter, Boyd, 16:297.
130. a young gentleman, Ford, 1:150.
131. Here certainly, Ford, 1:159.
131. the bastard, Nock, 182-183.
131. Hamilton's financial, Ford, 1:160-162.
134. I long, Ford, 5:326.
134. I am extremely, Chinard, 258.
134. I have a dozen, Cappon, 1:245-246.
135. I know not, Cappon, 1:248-249.
136. we are encompassed, Hirst, 284.
136. there may be, Padover, *Jefferson*, 204.
136. I was duped, Ford, 6:102.
136. When I came, Ford, 6:108-109.
137. which I am, Schachner, 500.
137. Since it has, Forman, 56-57.

Chapter XII
139. I had retired, Ford, 7:93.
139. I return, Cappon, 1:254.
139. I have no, Cappon, 1:263.
139. The house, Rosenberger, 41-42.
140. In our private, Ford, 7:14.
140. The little spice, Ford, 7:10.
140. No circumstances, Ford, 6:512.
142. I intreat you, Padover, *Jefferson*, 241.
142. Politics, a subject, Cappon, 1:259.
142. I have no, Ford, 7:94.
142. The idea, Ford, 7:116-117.

Chapter XIII
143. The second office, Ford, 7:120.
143. My country, Padover, *Jefferson*, 246.
143. I thank you, Ford, 7:113-114.
143. the President, Chinard, 325.
143. I do not, Ford, 7:109.
144. scarcely a dry, Padover, *Jefferson*, 248.
144. temporizing, Chinard, 322.
144. Peace is, Ford, 7:149-150.
145. exchange the roar, Ford, 7:155.
145. I now see, Schachner, 596.
146. The question, Ford, 7:225.
146. To separate, Ford, 7:274.
146. Federalist reign, Padover, *Jefferson*, 258.
147. For my own, Ford, 7:283.
147. that these, Ford, 7:303.
147. The spirit, Ford, 7:373-374.
148. I do then, Ford, 7:327-329.
149. The first object, Ford, 7:329.
149. I know that, Padover, *Profile*, 117-118.

149. I promised you, Ford, 7:460.

Chapter XIV
151. A just, Ford, 8:8.
151. Called upon, Ford, 8:1-3.
153. My principles, Padover, *Jefferson*, 299.
153. My position, Ford, 8:76.
153. A person, Nock, 254.
153. whenever a man, Nock, 255.
153. The task, Nock, 255.
154. When we consider, Ford, 8:120.
154. For defence, Ford, 8:121.
154. A small force, Ford, 8:122.
156. it may be, Nock, 246.
156. The judiciary system, Ford, 8:123.
156. The judges, Cappon, 1:279.
156. fill their newspapers, Padover, *Jefferson*, 329-330.
156. Every word, Forman, 391.
157. You know, Padover, *Jefferson*, 330.
157. No experiment, Padover, *Jefferson*, 330.
157. no man, Padover, *Jefferson*, 331.
157. I cannot omit, Ford, 8:124.
157. I have never, Nock, 259.

Chapter XV
159. There is, Ford, 8:144, 145.
160. Kindly separated, Ford, 8:3.
161. The suspension, Ford, 8:204.
161. We stand, Ford, 8:173.
161. to defray, Schachner, 724.
161. the fever, Ford, 8:188.
161. You possess, Ford, 8:190-191.
162. An intelligent, Ford, 8:201-202.
162. The expedition, Ford, 8:492.

163. Our circumstances, Ford, 8:205.
163. Peace is, Schachner, 736.
163. Never was, Padover, *Jefferson*, 341.
164. Others may, *Domestic Life*, 302-303.
164. her, who, Cappon, 1:269.
164. Had you, Cappon, 1:268-269.
164. I will not, Cappon, 1:282.

Chapter XVI
165. we have, Ford, 8:343.
165. But who, Ford, 8:344.
165. I shall now, Ford, 8:347-348.
166. Burr's enterprise, Ford, 9:7.
166. The fact, Ford, 9:41.
166. there is not, Ford, 9:111.
167. unpleasant views, Ford, 8:391.
167. our coasts, Ford, 8:389.
168. The whole world, Hirst, 439.
169. The alternative, Mayo, 279.
170. You Infernal, Padover, *Jefferson*, 354.
170. Oh! for, Chinard, 458.
170. present paroxysm, Padover, *Jefferson*, 354.
170. In truth, Padover, *Jefferson*, 354.
170. I think one, Ford, 9:201.
170. to postpone, Chinard, 458.
170. I have thought, Chinard, 461.
170. I thought Congress, Ford, 9:244.
171. Of you, Ford, 9:251.

Chapter XVII
173. I wished not, Schachner, 887.
173. Never did, Forman, 118.
173. I have, Padover, *Jefferson*, 362.
174. All my wishes, Boyd, 12:26.
174. So I hope, Nock, 281.
174. No occupation, Mayo, 287.

174. I am retired, Forman, 119-120.
175. devoured by, Padover, *Jefferson*, 364.
175. cannibal press, Chinard, 468.
176. the decays, Chinard, 514.
176. an old, Chinard, 530.
176. I always, Cappon, 2:284.
176. This is enough, Ford, 9:300.
177. two Pieces, Cappon, 2:290.
177. a letter, Cappon, 2:291-292.
179. Would you, Cappon, 2:464.
179. I hesitate, Cappon, 2:483.
179. Crippled wrists, Cappon, 2:599.
179. the most effectual, Nock, 313.
179. if a nation, Nock, 313-314.
179. do not generally, Ford, 10:96.
180. This institution, Ford, 10:174.
181. The plan, Mayo, 326-327.
182. The question, Ford, 10:277.
183. to extend, Padover, *Jefferson*, 392.
183. long and serene, Ford, 10:375.
183. if he lived, Padover, *Jefferson*, 404.
183. The first thing, Padover, *Jefferson*, 404.
183. When lately, Mayo, 321.
184. You know, Ford, 9:486.
186. If refused, Ford, 10:377.
186. But why, Ford, 10:377.
186. No cent, Hirst, 571.
186. has been, Cappon, 2:614.
186. We shall meet, Cappon, 2:610.
186. Independence forever, Cappon, 2:559.
187. May it be, Ford, 10:391-392.
189. was calm, *Domestic Life*, 427.
189. This is, *Domestic Life*, 428.
189. he sat up, *Domestic Life*, 428.
189. Thomas Jefferson, Adams, 1:636.